AF593299

# Testing the Wicket

*To my wife Winnie*
*and to Michael Crane*
*for his encouragement*

# Testing the Wicket

## From Trent Bridge to Lord's

JIM FAIRBROTHER

and

REGINALD MOORE

PELHAM BOOKS
LONDON

First published in Great Britain by Pelham Books Ltd
44 Bedford Square London WC1B 3DU
1984



British Library Cataloguing in Publication Data
Fairbrother, Jim
Testing the wicket.
1. Cricket grounds
I. Title II. Moore, Reginald
688.7'6358'0680924 GV927

ISBN 0 7207 1399 4

Typeset by Cambrian Typesetters, Aldershot, Hants
Printed and bound by Billings & Sons, Worcester

## ACKNOWLEDGEMENTS

The authors are grateful to the following for permission to use copyright material in this book: the *Sunday Telegraph* and Tony Lewis for the extract on page 21, Fred Titmus and Stanley Paul Ltd for the extract from *Talk of the Double* on page 110, the *Daily Mail* and Peter Smith for the extract on pages 110 and 111 and Christopher Martin-Jenkins and *The Cricketer* for the extract on page 7.

# CONTENTS

## LIST OF ILLUSTRATIONS



### PHOTOCREDITS

*Central Press 20; Roy Chaplin 10; Daily Star 21; Patrick Eagar 3, 4, 5, 6, 11, 16, 17, 18; Ken Kelly 12; Nottingham Guardian 2; Morley Pecker 25; Leslie Stinton & Partners 14.*

# FOREWORD

The publication of *Testing the Wicket* coincides with Jim Fairbrother's retirement, after sixteen years, from his post as head groundsman at Lord's. In the intervening period he has certainly had his problems. For instance, in 1983 the worst April and May on record prevented any play in all but a few matches – to be followed by a distinctly un-English heat wave which, despite all efforts, produced cracks in the square. Christopher Martin-Jenkins, editor of *The Cricketer*, concluded his report on England's Third Test match against New Zealand thus:

'Much talk during the match was centred on the pitch. There was some evidence to suggest the return of the notorious Lord's ridge of the sixties. . . .

'This is the second to last season for one of the best-loved characters at Lord's, that ruddy-faced groundsman with the ready smile, Jim Fairbrother. It was not the best strip he has prepared, but let it not be forgotten that he had to contend with a long spell of dry weather after a very wet May, and that in the last two seasons he has been judged by a panel of experts the groundsman of the year.'

Nevertheless, 1983 saw the toppling of the pride of West Indian batting by long-odds India and Somerset's last-over triumph in the NatWest Cup final. But for Jim 1981 was the great year – his county of birth, Nottinghamshire won the County Championship for the first time in fifty-two years.

Everyone who knows Jim pays tribute to his dedication, his generosity and his kindliness. Of late he has not been in the best of health and I am sure I can speak for thousands of cricketers, of all shapes, sizes and degrees, in wishing him a full recovery and, with his wife Winnie, many happy years ahead.

Reginald Moore

# PART I
## *ON THE SQUARE*

# 1

# LORD'S ON THE BIG DAY

Saturday. The third day of the second Test match between England and Australia. England hold the Ashes but having lost at Trent Bridge are one down with four to go. In reply to England's first innings total of 311 Australia are 10 without loss. And I am out in the middle dressed not in my working clothes but in a dark suit to give the proceedings a bit of ceremony, waiting by the wicket covers. Waiting on the weather.

The dove-grey clouds, among them an occasional evil-looking wad of black, are sailing slowly over us from the north-west, almost directly over the gap between the members' pavilion and the Warner stand.

The precious wicket itself and the immediate surrounds have been under cover since the previous day. Alec Gull, my very capable number one, and our permanent staff of six, buttressed by nearly a dozen additional helpers, mostly MCC young cricketers, wait with me.

There is a steady flow of incoming spectators and I know that thousands more are queuing right up St John's Wood Road and Wellington Place. Obviously they have loosed the shackles of the working week for that's just how they look – the young of both sexes in bright T-shirts and jeans or slacks, their picnic lunches in bags slung over the shoulder or carried in shiny little picnic cases. Their outbursts of laughter and buzz of talk reach us from all over the ground as they settle on the terraces or on the grass behind the boundary boards – three or four thousand are accommodated there on this big day.

These days several matches every season are big occasions;

the NatWest Cup Final, the final of the Benson & Hedges competition and, if Middlesex are in the running for the title, the last Sunday John Player league match. Club and village cricketers play the finals of their national competitions here too and these are always well attended. The University and Eton and Harrow matches are still part of Lord's rare tradition.

But a Test Match, particularly with the 'old enemy', has a pull of its own. Even people who seldom watch cricket, except perhaps on television, come along to try to get in, if they haven't wheedled tickets out of their cricketing friends beforehand. And that's why, as I shuffle about in the middle, I am keeping my fingers crossed. Personally I want everyone here to enjoy the skills and excitement of the game, not to have to worry about whether the conditions are fit to play.

Up to now the summer has been so utterly predictable in its unpleasantness: a soaking May, with match after match abandoned, and in June, except for a day here and there, hardly a glimmer of sun through forbidding clouds. And yesterday the familiar demons of rain and bad light had done their best – or worst – to fell a fascinating tussle.

Today we know already from the local forecast, received as usual from the RAF weather bureau at Northolt, that we must expect drizzle – but it shouldn't last for more than half an hour. Expectation of some rain is why we still have the covers on and are ready for action when it comes, immobile as we may look while we wait and see.

Ah, here it is. A slight breeze fans it gently and wetly across our faces. The clock tower tells us it is still only a quarter to eleven. So if this is all we are going to get the start of play need not be delayed. But now the umbrellas are going up. Spectators are hastening not strolling to their seats and for positions on the grass. Trying not to worry too much I watch an Aussie supporter lope in, parading his felt hat with those little bobbles dangling from the brim to keep off the bush flies. And now here's a plump fellow garbed in a Union Jack and waving a similar flag. (Sad to report that sometime later we saw him being gently conducted out of the ground by a policeman, excessive patriotism or over-imbibing having prompted him to run across the playing area and interrupt play.)

Out here in the middle we can feel the tension building up. Will we be able to make the eleven-thirty start as scheduled? It is now ten past the hour and the drizzle is thickening. Could even the RAF weather experts be wrong?

We now have extra flat sheets to extend cover of the bowlers' run-ups. I have a word with Alec and he calls on a few more ground-staff boys to join us. I signal the tractor driver to drag out the extra covers.

The forecast was so positive that the rain would last no more than half an hour that I am still fairly optimistic the game will re-commence on time. But the minutes tick by, the rain, though gentle, continues and I don't have to look around to know that the lads share my feelings. Slight but persistent rain is perhaps even more exasperating than a brisk shower. The conditions are so nearly right yet we have to stand about like mugs as if the whole situation is somehow our own doing. We are always aware that the spectators regard us as interlopers between them and the players. If we weren't here the game would magically begin.

As it happens, the drizzle *is* lessening . . . and almost ceases. The clouds appear to lift, it becomes a little brighter. We move around in relief.

However, enough rain has fallen to compel us to get those extra covers on, for any more of it, with the bowlers' longer run-ups uncovered, will certainly mean further delay to the start. The covers have been unhooked from the tractor and we get to work unrolling them.

Groans from the crowd are audible.

Our caution is justified when another black cloud sends down what, despite the RAF, feels like steady rain. The umbrellas in the crowd, which had scarcely shown wetness, are soon glistening and the rain is dropping off them. Somebody fetches my anorak for which I am very grateful.

It is eleven twenty-five, the moment when I should be setting the stumps and waiting at the wicket to hand over to the umpires, approaching down the pavilion steps. Instead, however, we are still battling to get those extra sheets finally rolled out. They are very heavy, I can assure you, and when we have a real downpour and they have collected a lot of water, even our tractor puffs and blows in its efforts to tow each one to its match site behind the advertisement boards at the Nursery end.

By now Colonel Stephenson, MCC secretary to cricket and my immediate boss – a genial and generous man, though he will chip me for saying it – has joined us. The red rose in his buttonhole strikes a brave note. As if he has commanded it, the rain gives over, but for good?

More waiting and then the umpires, Ken Palmer and Don Oslear, walk out, but with no white coats over their blazers. Over the public address system the crowd has just been informed that now it has stopped raining, and in view of Northolt's forecast of no further rain, play will begin as soon as the pitch has been cleared.

So, with a wary glance up at the heavens, we get on with removing everything that such a short time ago we had rushed on to the table. Ken and Don are inspecting the mobile wicket covers to make sure no water has crept in underneath them.

Colonel Stephenson puts his back into it with the rest of us – a line of more than a dozen men and lads, rolling up each flat sheet as we trudge over them.

A few weak cheers accompany our efforts but I think I know what is being said. 'What a silly arrangement. How primitive! And it's taking so long. There must be better ways of covering and uncovering the wicket. Know what they do at Edgbaston? They've got a huge tarpaulin operated mechanically that covers the whole ground – and it takes only a few minutes.'

How I long to be able to tell them that Bernard Flack, Warwickshire's head groundsman, is by no means certain that his £50,000 polyethlene cover is the final answer. Removing any cover which might bear a million gallons of water is the tricky part of it. It might take only nine or ten minutes for two men, aided by hydraulic motors, to unroll it, but the bigger the cover, the more men you need to remove it and the greater the risk of some of that water spilling on to the wicket. A great innovation, certainly, but with our big drop from the Father

Time stand to the Tavern it will be doubtful if we can ever use one, though of course we went to the demonstration and are closely watching the results in actual match use.

And I am sure others are piping up with: 'Why aren't they using the Whale? That new roller thing from Australia. They've got it on loan from the Oval – trust the Oval to be way ahead of sleepy old Lord's. And the Surrey groundsman Harry Brind's with them to operate it. Come on, don't bother with those ridiculous sheets – next time leave the table as it is and just have the Whale to mop it all up.'

True enough, Harry and the Surrey CCC have been as co-operative as ever. And yesterday, Friday, the second day of the match it was used on the outfield, particularly the Tavern side, which, as I've said, is always our problem. The machine is another excellent innovation and of such practical use to us that we already have one on order, having emerged from what our questioner suggests is a permanently comatose state.

Now it is almost five minutes past noon. Don Oslear and Ken Palmer emerge from the pavilion at last in their white coats, to be followed soon after, and to a loyal cheer, by England in the field, looking quite sprightly. Then Graham Wood and John Dyson, sober and with every appearance of confidence though one knows quite well that even world-class batsmen are combating butterflies in the stomach at the thought of the savage deliveries that will meet them from morning-fresh fast bowlers.

The white gate is closed behind them; the match is on.

For me, indeed for everyone on the ground staff, it started so long ago – back last autumn. The Test match is always played on the strip in the middle of the square, directly in line with the white wicket gate of the pavilion, and when Colonel Stephenson and I plan the rotation of matches to be played on the eighteen wickets which is all the Lord's table takes, that is the one we mark in at once.

As I sit in my chair beside the Nursery end sightscreen, I think of all the wind and the rain, the mist and sun, the icy blasts and frost which it has endured – and the practical care and nursing it demands. Now, for the third day, it is being rigorously tested.

The progress of the game was fairly predictable, given some knowledge of players' form and abilities. Remembering Wood's 112 in the Cornhill Centenary Match the previous September I wasn't surprised that he not only defended his wicket successfully against the early ferocity of Bob Willis and Graham Dilley but also forged towards his half-century. And if he had to miss it, who better to effect it than Bob Taylor, recalled to the England team close on his fortieth year, with a superb dive to his right off Bob Willis.

Mine was among the English hearts that rose to Botham's dismissal of Dyson to a catch by David Gower – to be found, rather improbably, in the slips – and then Yallop's stumps spread-eagled by Dilley, making amends for a wayward line and far too many no-balls.

Kim Hughes and Alan Border were bound to be England's bugbear and with the crowd getting listless as the afternoon wore on and as the runs rattled up on the scoreboards I found it difficult to understand why Botham was ignoring John Emburey, who had been brought into the English side specifically to disturb such a partnership. When he was given the ball he took a wicket with his second ball, Willis falling over backwards in the deep to take a skyscraper from Hughes.

At that point it seemed *just* likely that we might have Australia out for under 200, giving England a commanding lead, but their tail-enders seem so much more reliable than ours – they bat with tremendous concentration and determination and when stumps were drawn Rodney Marsh was still there on 43, with his partner, left-arm spinner Ray Bright, looking menacingly safe.

As we rushed on to rope in the square, so many spectators having already invaded the playing area, I had a feeling that the writing was on the wall. It would be another drawn game. This was the fifth meeting of England and Australia since I had come to work there in 1968. Including the 1977 Jubilee match, three had finished that way. I had never seen England bring off a victory but, like everyone else, had witnessed with some amazement Bob Massie whipping through our batting to take 16 wickets for 137 and give his side an easy eight wickets win in 1972.

With six draws against the other leading countries in the same period I think it could fairly be said that at Lord's we certainly have nothing against the batsmen.

On the first day of this match Trevor Bailey was saying on BBC radio, 'If it's anything like the wicket the University match was played on last week, it's going to be a perfect batting wicket,' Brian Johnston chipping in with, 'I gather the pitch has had no water on it since last Tuesday – that's about ten days ago. There are some little cracks in it but they won't affect play.' And Freddie Trueman mentioned what I'd said to him earlier in the week about there being a bit of bounce in it so the bowlers need not despair, while the batsmen could look to their stroke play. He added that in his own opinion the ball would turn later on in the match but not much.

Yet I believe on the last two days one or two of the commentators were talking of 'uneven bounce' at the Nursery end. Shades of the old ridge? My view is that the pitch is always said to be doing odd things when England are struggling but of no help at all to our bowlers when a batsman like Viv Richards or Clive Lloyd is slamming fours and sixes!

Not that I hold anything against the BBC commentary team. They are always very friendly and when I hear after the day's play how they single me out for praise, though never fogetting to spread it over my loyal ground staff whose work could easily be taken for granted, I feel quite embarrassed.

In the event the second Test match between England and Australia in July 1981 did turn out to be a draw.

At eleven o'clock on the final day England had resumed their second innings at 129 for two with Boycott on 47 and Gower on 38. After his customary early morning net practice Geoff had said to me: 'Now, Jim, I'm going to put the icing on the cake.' And of course I knew what he meant. Another 53 runs to his name in the scorebook and he would have made a century in his one hundredth Test match.

Although his partnership with David Gower prospered I thought he looked a little tired and strained, possibly because Ray Bright, with his looping spin, had been giving him rather a difficult time from the Nursery end.

When the total was 178, and they had put on 123, Dennis Lillee, off his short run, bowled one just wide of the off stump, Geoff thought about cutting it, the ball glided off his angled bat and it was in Rod Marsh's gloves.

And as for Ian Botham, with a duck in each innings and resigned and, or, deposed as England captain immediately after the match? I felt so very sorry for him because I had seen each phase of the development of his exceptional talent.

Before the game I had wished him luck.

'Well, I suppose I can always get a job back on your ground staff,' he said glumly. Then he added, with a touch of his old humour, 'I bet I'd be the highest paid member.'

For that was where his dazzling career had started. On our ground staff at Lord's.

How could anyone possibly have foreseen how dramatically, magically almost, Ian Botham's star would rise again. When he gave up the England captaincy immediately after the match at Lord's, and learnt from Alec Bedser, one of the selectors, that he would have been relieved of it anyway, it was scarcely surprising. Under him England had subsided heavily to the West Indies at home and abroad and, more to the point, his own marvellous flair for taking the opposition apart as a middle-order batsman and also operating successfully as a front-line swing bowler, seemed to have deserted him.

In interviews he himself still refused to acknowledge that the weight of captaincy might have something to do with his lapse of form. But the selectors were of the same mind as his critics and brought back Mike Brearley to lead England in the next three Test matches. Mike, bless him, for he is such a thorough-going sportsman, believed that he could guide Ian back to his former brilliance as an all-rounder, though the general opinion was that Botham had sunk too far below his best to recover his form that quickly.

Then came Headingley. The third Test of the six-match series with England still one down.

We felt that nothing like England's recovery in the third Test at Headingley could ever happen again in any Test series for many years to come. It was the rearguard action of all rearguard actions.

But we hadn't reckoned with a resurgent Ian Botham. And he is the man I am writing about because I so well remember him as an eager, boisterous lad among all those other MCC ground-staff hopefuls back in the early seventies. Mike Gatting was with us about the same time and was generally considered to have rather more promise than Ian.

The coaches were certainly not wrong about Mike, he has already shown his grit and accomplished technique as his country's No. 5 and a snapper-up of half-chances in the field, but I think we all understimated the Cheshire boy.

England's second victory of the series at Edgbaston on a wicket of Bernard Flack's that all the pundits voted a perfect batting strip was by no means wholly due to Ian Botham.

I would give points to Mike Brearley's captaincy, particularly for his timing of the bowling changes and the field placings that again denied Australia the slightest chance of breaking through; to Bob Willis for softening up their attack; to John Emburey for his 6 for 82 over both innings and his not out innings of 37 in England's second, an example to the more acknowledged batsmen who had gone before him; and to Mike Gatting who dominated the middle order.

But of our current crop of Test cricketers who but Ian Botham could have polished off an Australian innings that at 144 for 5 still looked capable of reaching 151 without too much trouble?

Five wickets for one run. And among them the elegant and seemingly unshakeable Martin Kent, veteran Test men Rod Marsh and Dennis Lillee, and Ray Bright, the night watchman England had earlier laboured to dismiss. Any one of them, you would have said, was quite capable of making the necessary 37 runs off his own bat.

On the Nursery ground at Lord's we shall have to erect a notice 'TO IAN BOTHAM: NO VACANCY'. Whatever his future, he had already gone to the highest school and conquered it.

# 2

# WATER, WATER EVERYWHERE

Rain is the groundsman's friend. Without spring showers, as in the drought periods we experienced in 1975 and 1976, ground preparation is made immensely more difficult. The sprinklers are in constant use over a wide area but it is still a struggle between the fresh young grass shoots and the hot dry winds which are the worst attackers.

Although we Britons groan and complain about the grey skies and resultant soakings during the average months of February, March and April cricketers know that, with any luck, it means they will be treading green springy turf in the summer months.

Bowlers, in particular, curse the hard grounds of a really torrid season. The sprigs of their boots are torn out, their feet get sore and on an unyielding wicket batsmen are that much harder to dismiss.

But we are talking of gentle rain and the rain that fell on Lord's cricket ground in the afternoon of Friday, 3 August 1979 was far from gentle. It was a tropical downpour. It came down in sheets. It lashed our faces. You couldn't see anything but rain. It came thick and fast, bouncing up from the already sodden turf with a kind of devilish glee.

It was the second Test match, against India, England having won the first at Edgbaston with a day to spare. And it was one of those big occasions for which Lord's is always well primed. My ground staff of six implemented by club and ground lads to about eighteen; all the catering laid on; MCC members, including many former England players, eager to study form; a full house of spectators on the terraces, in the Father Time, Warner, Tavern and Mound stands.

On the previous day enough light rain had fallen to interrupt play several times in the morning. We had lost something like three-quarters of an hour.

Venkat must have regretted winning the toss, though in fact even this part of the day's cricket was queered up. We heard that Mike Brearley believed he had given India first knock while the Indian captain thought he'd won the toss and made the choice himself.

Under heavy and uncertain skies English medium-pacers can do a lot with the ball, both in the air and off the wicket, and Botham and Hendrick gave the Indians an uncomfortable time. They were all out for 96, Ian bagging five wickets and Mike's two being those of Vengsarkar and Viswanath who, on another day, might have been worth at least fifty each.

So we came to Friday with Geoff Boycott and Graham Gooch at the wicket and 53 for one on the board, Mike Brearley having gone for 12 to a catch off the fiery Kapil Dev the evening before.

England's batsmen didn't look much happier than the Indians had been. Boycott collected his usual tally from deft strokes through the slips and off his legs and reached 32 but then Ghavri, left-arm over, induced him to flick at a ball that was moving away from him and we were 60 for two. Next to go was Gooch for 10. Probably because he'd taken rather a long time over it he launched himself into a straight attacking shot, and the ball beat him and went through. Seventy-one for three.

Derek Randall joined David Gower but only briefly. It was ten past noon and the skies were darkening. Dicky Bird and Ken Palmer, the umpires, had no hesitation in bringing the players off. And we all sensed that this was only the beginning of a truly wretched day. We rushed on with the covers and it was just as well for the rain was so heavy you could hardly see through it.

Towards one o'clock the shower passed over and the sun came out. Which brought our first session of mopping and tidying up. We didn't do too badly. The captains and the umpires discussed it after a few words with me and it was decided that play might be re-started after tea. There would be a further inspection at half-past three.

But the news from the Met. Office and the RAF station at Northolt, who alert us to more local conditions, wasn't good. There was another, greater build-up of rain cloud coming our way. And it certainly did.

What a blessing that Test wickets are now allowed to be covered when necessary in the duration of a match – otherwise there would have been no chance of any play on that previous track even for the whole of the next day.

Tony Lewis, that likeable ex-Glamorgan and England skipper, did us proud in his report on the day for the *Sunday Telegraph*.

'After the floods,' he wrote, 'the calm. Only the rich green of the grass told the story of Friday's deluge, of how a long, slender pond had settled before the Tavern, and how the day had ended a zany aquatic jamboree, with spectators belly-flopping into pools which swamped the whole playing surface.

'Yet the calm belied the almost heroic rescue act performed by the Lord's ground staff.

'As Friday's storm broke they arrived with their covers and tarpaulins more quickly and in greater numbers than I have ever seen before. They were drenched to their skins but stuck to their tasks almost beyond the call of duty.'

Every groundsman gets a bit of stick at times, especially at a famous ground like Lord's, so I couldn't help feeling good at remarks like these. As I told Brian Scovell, who was also complimentary to me and the boys in the *Daily Mail*, it was the worst sight I'd seen in the eleven years I'd been at headquarters. And people who had been there all their lives said they had never seen the ground as bad as that.

I really did fear that the water swishing down the hill would get under the covers and on to the wicket. We threw down sandbags to divert it but when it went on coming I had to station some of the chaps to brush it away with brooms. It was like an onslaught.

Five years before, when England were hosts to Pakistan, we were using balloon-type covers. We couldn't peg them down too deep because it would have damaged the other wickets.

What happened? They just tried to take flight, and the water did come in on the track. The Pakistanis took it badly and their manager seemed to think we hadn't done our job properly. What you can do in these abnormal weather conditions depends entirely on your equipment.

By 1979 we had £30,000-worth of covers including two covers, which we laid flat on the turf, borrowed from Wimbledon. These enabled us to keep the Tavern side of the square much drier than ever before. Also, our present covers are lighter and modern tractors can get them out to the middle much quicker.

As we laboured on in the lashing rain memories of other such crises flitted across my mind. There was the day I spent some twenty years ago helping Harry Lowe, the Nottingham Forest groundsman, to try to rescue Forest's third round F A Cup-tie against Wolverhampton Wanderers. We used sponge mats to mop up water lying in the goalmouths and must have looked like donkeys on a treadmill.

It was January and it had been snowing for days. Then came the thaw – and the water.

We managed it, though. The match was played the following evening. Sportsmen always help one another and Forest and Nottingham County Cricket Club, where I had been assistant groundsman since 1952, were, and I am sure still are, the friendliest of neighbours.

Then I thought of Trent Bridge on the first day of England's second Test against Pakistan, in August 1967. The unfortunate visitors had been taken apart by Higgs and Arnold for 140. In the soft evening light Colin Cowdrey and young Geoff Boycott – how that man comes into all one's memories – arrived at the wicket to open for England.

Two overs were bowled and then the rain thrashed down. Within minutes pools appeared on the grass. We rushed out the covers, but all too late. In the gloom the ground which had once been a cricket area became a vast lake. Our tractor, wrote Brian Chapman in the *Daily Mirror*, 'resembled a tank abandoned on some soaked battlefield'.

Finally my mind went back to 1968, the season I joined the Lord's staff. It was the Test match against Australia, 'the old enemy'. More rain. Not likely! This time it was a freak hailstorm and so severe it covered the entire ground like a snowfall.

One man who couldn't have been sorry to get away into the shelter of the pavilion was Colin Milburn. That mighty seventeen-stone figure had been the object of a bouncer attack from Mackenzie and his 16 not out, out of a total of 53, had left him black and blue. His partner, needless to say, was that ever-present Yorkshireman. There had been rain earlier and the wicket was playing up like mad.

But a hailstorm . . . in June!

As we slipped and slopped about in what, at times, seemed a hopeless rescue attempt to give the Saturday crowd some part of the England *v.* India Test I wondered what fresh pranks the weather gods had in store for us. A mini typhoon or tornado?

However, one thing groundsmanship teaches you is patience and perhaps just a spot of wisdom. Everything, even tropical rain, passes. All we could do was being done. And tomorrow was another day.

Actually, that August day five years ago felt more like two days rolled into one. None of us got much sleep that night and two of my assistants had stayed out on the square, ready to give the alarm if it rained again.

Late the previous evening the umpires, Dicky Bird and Ken Palmer, had inspected the wicket before leaving the ground and were astonished that it was quite dry and no water had infiltrated.

I went back to my little house at the Nursery End but was up again at first light – that was about five o'clock – and told my staunch sentries to snatch some sleep while they could. I might add that it isn't the number of people that make an efficient staff, whether on the ground or elsewhere but their individual quality and dedication. And I've certainly had that in all my years at Lord's.

I took a stroll round the place. Luckily the drains and gutters had done their job. When I'd last seen the arbours –

those apartments in a kind of long shed behind the new indoor cricket school which are allotted to private parties during a match – they were under a good three feet of water as was the staff parking lot. All the pedestrian ways on the Tavern side had caught it and now it was still mucky but the flood water was dispersing quickly.

There was no time to linger. The weather forecast over the radio had sounded good and we had to clear the decks and start work on the outfield if the expected Saturday crowd of thirty thousand were to see any cricket.

My boys were already taking off the flat covers. These are fine in an emergency but we never keep them on longer than we have to; there is nothing static or dead about grass and when anything is laid flat upon it the blades sweat and such moisture turns grass yellow and makes it prone to disease.

Another thing is that the flat white sheets collect water and they have to be removed from the pitch with the utmost care so that the build-up of water on top of them doesn't overflow on to the grass.

We opened up the square, all the covers, except the two actually covering the precious strip, being trundled off. The sky was clearing from the east over Regent's Park Zoo and a breeze had sprung up. It was quite bright and we all felt stimulated. Gone were the doubts of the previous day. Now we really knew that providing there were no treacherous showers about we could indeed save the day.

Spiking and forking were the priorities. We had to let the air into the soggy patches. We mopped up the worst areas which, of course, were on the Tavern side and then got to work with the Pattisson spiking machine and hand forks.

MCC secretary Jack Bailey was early on parade and so were the umpires. But we had started even earlier and by the time they came out to inspect the damage, we had the motor mowers going and were 'dressing it up' – that is, mowing and rolling to make the 'breeds' which give such a smart appearance to any sports ground, the alternate stripes in our case parallel to the wicket.

When I'd chatted with them, and told them I thought play

was possible, I nipped back home for a cup of tea with my wife Winnie.

The sun greeted me as I came out again. The staff I had detailed to get some breakfast were on call in the mess room or finishing the rolling. Others were taking an early lunch, so they could be ready for any more work to get play started on time.

Mr Bailey and the umpires told me there would be an inspection at twelve-fifteen. Spectators were to be admitted and, if there was no further rain, play would start immediately after the inspection.

Almost everyone connected with the match was at Lord's well before eleven. Some of the players, Boycott among them of course, were already at the nets and the Test selectors had arrived.

I met Bishan Bedi, the great Indian spinner, by the nets. He looked at me mournfully. 'I thought you were a friend of mine,' he said. 'Couldn't you have left a few damp spots?'

England made 357 for 7 that day, David Gower making 82 in a typically delightful innings, Derek Randall 57 before being run out in a stop-go with Ian Botham, and Geoff Miller 52 not out.

Michael Melford, in the *Daily Telegraph*, considered that the Indians 'did not bowl badly on a pitch which played far better than one would have expected after it had spent so long under covers'.

# 3

# BOMB SCARE

Naturally, Saturday is the peak of a five-day Test match. People come to Lord's in a week-end mood, casually dressed, carrying lunch bags or baskets, the worries of the working week pushed to the back of their minds. And what an incentive it gives to the players to see the stands and terraces packed. They have even got used to the noise.

One side has usually batted for a day and a half leading up to it so that the Saturday crowd, having digested the previous days's newspaper reports and radio and television coverage, are eager to judge the strength or otherwise of the opposition.

Strictly in cricket terms the Monday and Tuesday sessions of play can be the most exciting of the whole match with the result constantly in doubt. For the teams and all the rest of us Saturday is the big day.

On Saturday, 25 August 1973 we thought we were lucky. The sun was beating down. There wasn't a cloud in the sky. It felt like high summer. And the flag flying over the dressing room to the right of the pavilion was that of the West Indies. This meant that as well as the usual chatter and laughter we had the clamour of a steel band, roars, whistles and catcalls. It may offend some cricketing diehards, who can remember when cricket was a game honoured with hush, but I must say that nowadays a series with the West Indies would seem very odd without it.

It was the final Test in a three-match series, England having also entertained New Zealand that year, and England were really up against it.

Over the first day and most of the second, West Indies had

accumulated a massive 652, declaring at that total with two wickets in hand. Rohan Kanhai, the skipper, had scored 157, big Clive Lloyd 63, Julien 121, Fredericks 51 and then there was Sobers. Gary's 150 not out was an unforgettable innings. England's bowlers Arnold, Willis, Underwood, Illingworth and Greig were all treated almost with disdain. When Gary had used up all the strokes in the book he added a few of his own creation. Whenever cricketers get together they still talk about it. These days, with Viv Richards showing the same kind of staggering improvisation, the two men are often compared. For me, Gary still has a slight edge, certainly as far as all-round ability goes. He was a brilliant fielder, again so is Viv, but I am sure that Viv would be the first to admit that his own genial spin cannot compare with the deadly pace and variety of Gary's bowling.

A total of 652 would have been enough to make any team quail. But England's batting looked formidable enough on paper. It read: Boycott (Yorkshire), Amiss (Warwickshire), Luckhurst (Kent), Hayes (Lancashire), Fletcher (Essex), Greig (Sussex), Illingworth (Leicestershire), Knott (Kent), Arnold (Surrey), Willis (Warwickshire), Underwood (Kent).

However, on that Friday we lost three wickets for only 88, including Geoff Boycott for 4 and Brian Luckhurst for a single. There was no Holding, Roberts, Garner or Marshall to blame in those days: that menacing quartet was yet to come. But Holder, Boyce and Sobers, supported by Lance Gibbs's accurate offspin, were quite good enough to urge most of the England batsmen into fatal errors. In the end catches accounted for all of them.

So that glorious Saturday morning, although I had my full complement of helpers, always available to swell the ground staff for the big match, it looked as if we would have little to do except faithfully man the Nursery end sight-screens and be absolutely ready to do the necessary sweeping, line marking and tidying up of the bowlers' ends when England's first innings finally petered out.

As usual, the luncheon interval was taken at one-thirty and forty minutes later out came the buoyant West Indians to polish off the home side now reduced to the tail-enders.

Surprisingly perhaps, though it would not be the first Test innings in ruins that Bob Willis and Derek Underwood had shown courage and obstinacy in propping up, our last pair resisted all attempts to dislodge them.

At half-past two they were still there and I was sitting with my lads among the equipment we had expected to be using long before that.

'Well, you know what to do,' I said to my assistants Alec and Mike. 'It can't be long now but I must just stretch my legs.'

I was strolling behind the Mound Stand when I met one of the pavilion attendants. He seemed quite out of breath.

'Jim,' he panted, 'Jim, you're wanted, wanted in the committee room by Mr Griffith. He says it's most – most urgent. And will you come at once.'

'What is it?' We hurried together towards the Grace Gate.

'I can't say. I mean, I don't know. But Mr Griffiths . . . he wants you right away.'

It was all very mysterious. There was always close liaison between the MCC secretary and myself but never with quite this urgency.

'Well, take it easy,' I said, quickening my pace. 'I'll get along but we don't want you bursting a blood vessel or something.'

As I passed the newspaper sellers and went on by the Members' Stand I had to make my way through groups of policemen, and there certainly seemed more of them than usual. I couldn't figure out what on earth had happened.

The MCC committee room at Lord's is on the Tavern side of the pavilion below the home dressing-room. Billy Griffith's answer to my knock came at once and he was very brisk.

The room was crowded, mostly with police officers. I recognized our local Chief Inspector. But there were also plain clothes men, all looking very grim and some were edgy.

Mr Griffith wasted no time with introductions.

'Jim,' he said, 'sad news. We've got to stop the game.'

'Stop the game!' I couldn't help repeating it. 'What – on a perfect day like this.'

'We've had a phone call. A bomb's been planted here. Of

course they wouldn't say exactly where, though. The police are going to search every inch of the ground. It means clearing everyone out till they've finished. Your job, Jim, is to save that wicket. I want you to go back and get those covers on.'

I said, 'Right, sir. But what about the spectators? On a perfect day like this . . . the West Indians – they won't know what to make of it. There'll be a riot.'

Billy Griffith said, 'Leave them to me. At the right moment I'll be speaking to them over the public address.'

He went on to say that the twelfth man had already been sent out on some excuse but actually to warn the umpires and Rohan Kanhai as to what was going on and how the MCC administration intended to cope with it.

At a signal from the pavilion Charlie Elliott, the senior umpire, would pocket the ball. 'And that's when you get the covers on like lightning, Jim. Off you go.'

Just as I got to the door he asked, 'Oh, Jim – don't talk about it. We don't want any panic.'

Clattering down the stairs I remembered the last crisis when we were under attack before. It was in the winter of 1969, with the South African tour to start in spring '70.

England's tour of South Africa in 1968–9 had been cancelled due to the objection of South Africa's politicians to the inclusion of Basil D'Oliviera in our party, and the anti-apartheid demonstrators in this country had made all kinds of threats to interfere, if not altogether to prevent, the Test series over here.

The question of whether sport should be made the pawn of politics is still being debated. Most cricketers and cricket followers were saddened that the game itself should be so menaced. The South African cricketers themselves were always popular over here and since the international split a good many of them have played happily and successfully in various county sides – with and against West Indians, Indians and Pakistanis.

But in the early part of 1970 it had been part of my job to supervise the erection of barbed wire all round the table, with searchlights at strategic points. The boys and I had to be constantly on sentry duty, as it were.

Now I was hurrying off to do a very difficult job indeed. As I came round by the terraces I glanced at my watch and checked it with the clock. It was twenty to three. The sun shone down and the more sober spectators were blissfully bathing in it. The West Indian supporters were a little quieter than usual but only because they couldn't quite understand why their bowlers, so devastating before, were allowing Willis and Underwood to meet ball with bat. They should have been packed off to the pavilion long ago.

'Still staying put,' Alec said drily as I came up to my group.

'Never mind,' I said. 'Come over here a moment, will you. You too, Mike.'

I wasn't going to tell the others, but it would have been impossible to get the job done properly if my numbers one and two were kept in the dark. They would have thought I'd gone mad.

'Just the wicket covers,' I told them 'and we've got to be out there to make a ring round the track. The rest of the boys will know what's up soon enough when Mr Griffith gets on the p.a.'

Now came the worst part. As we were preparing the covers, making them as light as possible so that they could be rolled on at speed, the West Indian spectators on the terraces behind us gave us a good share of their attention.

'What you want with the covers, man?'

'Hey now, beer gone to yo' head. Put them things away.'

'See that sun up there? What you doin', man?'

But soon we were ready, poised like sprinters on the mark.

It was the end of an over. With a glance towards the pavilion Charlie Elliott nodded and swiftly popped the ball into one of his cavernous pockets. Led by Rohan Kanhai, the players walked steadily, purposefully toward the pavilion. And just as a huge hum of amazement went up from the crowd and trumpets and a steel clatter thundered out, Billy Griffith's voice came over the public address. It was necessary for the whole ground to be cleared immediately. The quicker people would leave their seats and get outside the ground in orderly fashion, the sooner play could be resumed.

Everyone left their places all right, even as we were haring out with the covers. But unfortunately most of the West Indians decided that the playing area was far enough to go, and they were soon joined by thousands of others.

The covers and my boys around them were protection enough for the Test wicket – but what about the other strip we had prepared for the important Gillette Cup Final to be played the following weekend? But with thousands of spectators now gathered on the grass there was nothing we could possibly do about it.

All the same I raced toward the pavillion to see if Mr Griffith had any further instructions. As I ran up the steps I saw one of the officials pointing to the middle.

'Look – Dicky Bird – are they stopping him from getting back?'

Sure enough, that perky little umpire, the man with the jaunty tilt to his hat and now as well known to cricket watchers as any Test player, was sitting astride one of the covers surrounded by West Indian supporters who were chanting 'No-ball Bird, no-ball Bird!' Just as obviously they were referring to his strictness on the front-foot-placing of the Caribbean bowlers who had already given away more than a dozen runs through their eagerness to get to the England batsmen.

At that moment Kanhai scrambled past us.

'Don't worry, I'll get him.'

What a wise move that was. Only the West Indian captain could command enough respect from the jeering fans to prise Dicky away from their slightly unwelcome attention. I am sure they would not have harmed him but all the same it was an uncomfortable position for him to be in. Besides, his rightful place was with Charlie Elliott back in the umpire's room.

It was an extraordinary scene: the terraces and stands now empty except for uniformed policemen and the bomb squad hopping over the seats and looking everywhere. And as a centrepiece the milling crowd obscuring the acres of lawn that were one's daily work. How I prayed they would do no permanent harm to that Gillette Cup Final strip!

Of course the bars had been closed and the staff were

sitting in the gardens at the back of the pavilion. Had the telephone caller told Mr Griffith which terrorist organisation he represented? I didn't know but the IRA had been very busy in London that year and I thought that most probably it was them.

The waiting was long drawn out: it seemed like hours. But in fact only just over an hour had passed when we were told the search was over. Nothing had been found.

Again I was called to the committee room for a conference to discuss if or when play would be resumed. Jack Bailey, the assistant secretary, and Mr Gaby, the club superintendent were there; so were Ray Illingworth and Rohan Kanhai and of course the umpires.

It was decided that play would re-start at half-past four. Over the public address the spectators both inside and outside the ground were invited to return to their seats – if they so wished. Obviously the MCC could not guarantee that nothing more would happen and there must have been plenty of crossed fingers. I found it surprising how many people had waited on.

Even more surprising was the splendid reaction to Mr Griffith's plea to everyone on the playing area that they should make sure to leave nothing behind them on the pitch, otherwise there would be further delay for rubbish to be cleared up. Hardly a plastic container or a cigarette packet was left there and punctually at four-thirty the West Indians trotted out again and Bob and Derek came to the crease.

What must have helped was a further announcement that in view of the time lost because of the emergency close of play would be at seven instead of six-thirty and on the Monday the match would continue half an hour earlier than usual – at eleven o'clock.

None of this was much good to England, however. We were out for 233 and the follow-on was enforced. And by the end of the day we had lost Boycott, Amiss and Knott for a total of 42.

I wasn't sorry to get back to my house overlooking the

Nursery ground. Everything was quiet now but the excitement of the day was still throbbing in my head.

'Feel like a cup of tea?' came my wife Winnie's voice from the kitchen.

Oh yes, indeed. Those were the most normal words that Saturday had offered me.

But on the Monday I had a very pleasant surprise. Jim Swanton, in the *Daily Telegraph*, wrote:

'A word of congratulation, by the way, to Jim Fairbrother on producing an absolutely ideal wicket, fast and true, and equally rewarding to bold batsmanship and fine bowling. Conditions are never precisely similar, but he should preserve the recipe for circulation to groundsmen.'

As I hope to show in the following chapters, the groundsman and his staff are not always favoured with such laudatory comments!

# 4

## AN INVITATION

Isn't it strange how an ordinary sort of day, a day that at the time seems very much like hundreds of other days, can change your whole life?

In 1952 I worked for the Nottingham Corporation Parks in Lenton Park and I liked the job. Lenton, like all the streets crowded into a square mile or so south of Castle Rock, is all streets and houses and shops, and everyone's grateful for a few acres of parkland.

We had a small cricket table, two bowling greens and a children's playground and I was happy enough doing my bit to keep the park clean and fresh. When I was demobbed from the service after the Second World War I had no wish to work in an office or to go back to the timber works where I'd been before joining up in '39.

On this particular morning I was clearing the leaves off the paths and grass. A congenial task, really, even in November mist. We'd done all the necessary tidying up and re-seeding of the bowling greens and cricket squares. Given a fairly mild run-up through November and December to the New Year the young grass would have a chance to root and settle whatever frost and wild winds and thrashing rain came on us later.

I was sweeping the leaves into heaps ready for the barrow and thinking how lucky I was to be in the open air and not tied to a desk or a machine, when I happened to glance up and see a tall soldierly figure walking towards me.

He was no stranger. Almost every morning he walked his dog in the park. His name was Edwin Alfred Marshall and I knew quite a lot about him. He lived in what to me was a grand house called the Old Priory just off the park. He was married, played a good game of golf and years ago he'd captained Nottinghamshire's second eleven after a spell with the firsts.

Usually, he gave me a cheery and brisk 'Morning, Jim,' and went on his way but today he stopped. I nodded, smiled and went on with my work.

'You know, Jim,' he said thoughtfully, after watching me a while, 'you shouldn't be doing this. You're worth something better, a job with more authority. You've done very well here – but don't you ever think of advancing yourself?'

To be honest, I didn't know what to say to this, so I just went on sweeping, though a bit shakily, I must admit.

Mr Marshall rested on his stick.

'Look, what I'm talking about is Trent Bridge. We could do with someone like you over there. I've got a committee meeting coming up later this week. Ask for a bit of time off and I'll pick you up and take you along. Come and see what you think of us. I'll show you around and bring you back after the meeting. It won't take long.'

I was flummoxed. But I gave him my address on the Apsley estate, thanked him and gazed after him as he strode off.

That enclosure over the river from us had a proud place on the roll of famous Test grounds. Lord's, the Oval, Old Trafford, Headingley . . . Trent Bridge. When I was about twelve I'd been lucky enough to go there often. Those were the years of the Depression and although both my parents were hard workers they wouldn't have been able to give me enough pocket-money to cover visits to Trent Bridge.

But my special friend of the time was more fortunate. His father had a secure job as a fireman at Boots factory. And his mother, when she heard that we wanted to spend the day watching Nottinghamshire, not only gave her son the fares and admission money, but would say, 'And here's yours, Jimmy. Now look after yourselves. And come back as soon as it's over.'

Thinking back, it occurs to me that she might have been glad to see the back of us because we were always up to things like taking a dip in the canal or chasing each other all over her house. But that's ungenerous. Actually, I can see her as a kind of goddess of plenty.

So we saw most of the great cricketers of the thirties. Our own George and John Gunn, and Harold Larwood and Bill Voce, the fast bowlers who figured so prominently in the bodyline controversy of the 1932–3 series in Australia. Then, for the opposition there was the smart-looking Herbert Sutcliffe of Yorkshire, perky Patsy Hendren of Middlesex – he was such a cheerful little man that we couldn't help wishing him well – and that remarkable batsman and wicket-keeper, Leslie Ames of Kent.

That evening I talked it over with my wife Winnie. What had I got to lose, she said. I might just as well take advantage of such a kind offer and just go along and see. Trent Bridge . . . just imagine.

I knew exactly what she meant.

All the time Winnie and I were talking it over these things were crowding into my mind and I must admit it was difficult to separate the childhood magic from having to arrive at a decision for the person I now was – a man in his thirties with a wife and family.

I did say to Winnie, 'But I'm just a park gardener. What's Mr Marshall got in mind for me?'

'Wait and see,' she said, with that feminine logic which, quite rightly, pins a man down to the immediate situation. 'You can't see yourself as others see you. He's watched you. Likes the way you work.'

It was a cold, dank and rather foggy afternoon when Mr Marshall picked me up in his Riley and drove up Castle Boulevard past the John Player factory and the old grey rock, up the embankment and over the bridge into the cricket ground.

The familiar features were comforting: the Trent Bridge Hotel at the entrance in Bridgeford Road, the big scoreboard facing us across the lovely spread of green and Sir Julian Cahn's double-tiered stand backing on Radcliffe Road where sometimes I sat on a match day. Then there was the old-style members' pavilion which, many years before, my pal and I had viewed with awe.

What was so strange was to be in the ground out of season. Out in the middle a cluster of men still worked on the table. They were putting the finishing touches to some re-turfing.

'Come and meet Frank,' Mr Marshall said as we got out of the car.

The men looked up as we approached and one of them waved and strolled towards us.

'Here he is,' said Mr Marshall. 'Frank Dalling – Jim Fairbrother. Frank's our head groundsman and a mighty good job he does for us.' Then, to Frank: 'I told you I'd be bringing him along. Now I'm off – mustn't keep the Club and Ground waiting. Chairman's place is in the chair, eh?'

'Don't worry, sir,' said Frank, 'Jim can stay with me. I'd like a chat with him.'

'Ah, thought you'd say that.' Mr Marshall nodded vigorously. 'I'll leave him in your hands. And you'll show him around, won't you. Tell him all the nice things about the Bridge. I want him to stay with us. Shouldn't take long this meeting. Join you afterwards.'

We watched him stride purposefully to the pavilion and then Frank tapped me on the arm.

'Know that feller over there?'

The man he was indicating heard what he said and, straightening up, leaned on his fork and tilted his head with a laugh.

I recognised him at once. I'd never met him but had seen him often enough in his white flannels out here in the middle and photographs of him in action in the sports pages of the *Post*. Harold Butler, our opening bowler.

I could see him walking back to the pavilion end at the start of the other side's innings, determined, thoughtful, and then the quick turn-around, and a dashing figure as he gathered speed, then the final furious wheeling of the arms, the dropped left shoulder, the front foot stamped down, and the crouching follow-through with an eye for a possible caught-and-bowled.

He came up and we shook hands. I said something about

how we always looked to him for a quick breakthrough – and how often he managed it – but he only looked rueful.

'Not often enough,' he said. 'What can a ruddy bowler do on *this* –' gently heeling the immaculate grass. 'Takes the guts out of you. Best batting strip in the country. An opening bat *smiles* when he walks out here. And you can sweat blood trying to wipe that smile off his face.'

Then he grinned and gave a great snort.

'Still, we have our moments – eh, Frank?' And he nodded agreeably and went back to his work.

Frank had a word or two with the other men and then gestured that we should go on our way.

'Harold helps us out a bit in the winter,' he said, as we headed for the pavilion. 'Does this and that. It's a lean time for the pros – unless they've got an off-season job or run a sports shop or a newsagent's or something like that.'

Once we had started on our tour everything seemed to happen rather fast. Frank showed me his workshop. It was nicely laid out, all shipshape. I was familiar with most of the equipment though of course there were more cutters and rollers than I had ever seen in a workshop before.

Over a cup of tea in the mess room I gathered that Frank's brother Harry was ground superintendent which meant that he was responsible for the seating, the refreshment rooms, toilets and other amenities, and the staff to man the turnstiles.

We chatted with another Notts pro. Eddie Lowe, the wicket-keeper, who was doing a bit of repairing on the tall brick wall enclosing the ground, roamed the players' dressing rooms and umpires' toom, then we were in the members' pavilion gazing at an oil painting of a famous head groundsman of the past. I really couldn't take in the many other portraits of players and officials and the framed photographs of Test and county cricket action – it was all a bit much for me, as you can imagine.

Next thing I remember was Mr Marshall emerging from his committee meeting which had just broken up.

'So you've had a good look round,' he said cheerfully. 'Did Frank take care of you?'

I assured him I'd been treated royally.

'Good, good. Then how do you feel about it, Frank. D'you want him here?'

I believe Frank said I was a big strong chap and he was sure we'd get on very well.

It was quite dark outside. In the car Mr Marshall said, 'What do you think then, Jim. We want you on the ground staff as Frank's assistant.'

I said I certainly appreciated the offer which, for the moment, was rather overwhelming. Nottinghamshire was a great club, *my* club in fact. And Frank Dalling was a good fellow, I knew I could work with him all right. Not that I was unhappy under Mr Wing at Lenton – whatever I knew about park management I'd learnt from him.

'But I've got to talk it over with the wife – you understand, sir?'

He glanced at me, nodded, as we turned off the bridge and down the boulevard.

I felt I had to add that jobs were scarce and I was in one with a superannuation scheme which gave us some security.

'Oh, we can do just as well for you in that regard,' he said. 'All our chaps are in a pension scheme. What are you getting a week now?'

I told him, four pounds ten shillings, but I'd want seven pounds a week clear if I was making a move.

'That's no obstacle,' he said, and as he pulled up outside our house he suggested I should come to his office in Gregory Street just as soon as I had made up my mind.

Winnie was all in favour of acceptance – and my only reservation was the fairly natural one for a working-class chap in the early post-war years of wanting to make sure I would not be giving up a pleasant safe job for a plunge into the unknown. The war itself had been a big enough jolt out of building a proper working life for myself and the family.

'Slept on it then?' was Mr Marshall's opening remark when I saw him again the next day. But he was truly delighted that my answer to his proposition was, yes.

The following week, having telephoned the club for an appointment, I visited Trent Bridge again. And this time I met Mr H.A. Brown, the secretary, though to me he wasn't 'Mr' but 'Captain' Brown. However, that's another story.

# 5

# NO LONGER A GARDENER

Herbert A. Brown, Justice of the Peace . . . I knew him all right!

Talking things over with him, and finding myself actually engaged on the Trent Bridge ground staff, was like dealing with a member of the family – say, a favourite uncle whom I hadn't seen for some time. Why? Because some twenty years before I had joined the 22nd St Mary's company of the Boys' Brigade. Mr Brown had founded the company with the aid of a probation officer. He was our captain and that's what we always called him. I think of him as that to this very day.

What Captain Brown did for us was to obtain the use of an old warehouse in the city and put us through physical training. He also gathered enough equipment for us to play table tennis and to box and wrestle. Then it was over to the Victoria Baths for swimming. As for outdoor sport, he hired park pitches for our cricket and football matches.

In the Sneinton district where I was brought up the tiny houses were back to back, our only water supply came from the common tap in the yard and we used earth privies. Appalling living conditions compared with those of today.

But some of the better-off people – men like Captain Brown and Eddie Marshall – were almost a welfare state in themselves, without the form-filling.

Both my father and mother went out to work and I was the only child. We were a typical working-class family but none the worse for it. I can't remember ever being deprived of the basic necessities of life. I suppose it was a tight budget but my parents must have trained themselves to be careful with money. I think it's a pity that now the workers demand more and yet never seem to be satisfied.

My father was a twist-hand in the lace-making trade – Nottingham is famed for many things and that's one of them. In the 1920s that trade, like many others, began to feel the pinch but a whole new lace-making industry had started up across the Atlantic in Philadelphia and my father went over there to help set up the machinery for one of the concerns. He thought it would be for only a month or two; in fact, it was almost a year before we saw him again.

My mother worked as a french polisher at Adams & Shelton in Sussex Street. Hers was an eight-hour day Monday to Friday and four hours on Saturday. No one dreamed of a forty-hour week in those days, though the equalisation of work and leisure over the past forty years is a social revolution surely everybody supports.

Mother never seemed to stop working. She was hard at it well into her sixties. At that time of her life she found herself in demand at the big private houses in our district called the Park on the hill against Nottingham Castle.

The owners would go abroad for a month or two in the winter and that was when they liked to have their furniture polished. A chauffeur would call to take Mother off on her day's work and she would be given the keys to all the rooms and have the run of the house. When she had finished she would be driven home again. I think she rather enjoyed it.

When I came out of Captain Brown's room I felt for the first time since that day in Lenton Park with Eddie Marshall that I was taking the right step in exchanging a gardener's job for that of groundsman. Had I been over-cautious? Maybe. But your work is your life and I have never been one to take it lightly.

A fortnight later I was checking in at Trent Bridge and I soon found that things were a bit different from what I had been used to at Lenton Park.

I got to the ground in good time for an eight o'clock start. But although my new mates were also there promptly we didn't actually start work for half an hour. With several pros temporarily on the ground staff there was plenty of chat about the game we were serving. The mess room was alive with it.

For instance, there was our new scoreboard.

In the spring of the previous year Mrs Forman Hardy had officially handed it over to the club. It was in memory of her brother who had once owned the *Nottingham Guardian* and had always taken a great interest in Nottinghamshire County Cricket Club.

With this board Nottinghamshire were certainly leading the way among the county clubs. It was electrically operated to give the batsmen's scores, the innings total and any extras. The names of both the batting and fielding sides would go up there, and only the bowling analyses, how the previous batsmen had come out and the runs they had scored were hand-operated.

All that Nottinghamshire needed now was a winning streak for in 1952 they had propped up the County Championship table and, from what I could gather, no one thought they deserved to be in that lowly state.

It was a hard December with a bitter north-east wind blasting through the gaps between the stands but while there was little to be done on the playing area, we were given plenty of work.

With Coronation Year and the Australian tour ahead, all the spectator benches had to be cleaned and re-painted. Fortunately, we were able to do this indoors after we had collected them – in a building at the Fox Road end which was also used by the West Bridgford company of the Boys Brigade.

Three of us constituted the permanent ground staff – Frank Dalling, Ron Allsopp and myself. Ron was to succeed Frank as head groundsman and we are still firm friends. We had three pros to help us in the off season (Ron Giles, the club's opening bat was among them) and we could call upon some juniors.

But having a caterer on the ground – all the year round in the case of Trent Bridge for many local functions were held there – certainly has its advantages. Early on that first day I'd said to Frank that if it was all right with him I'd go off in lunch-break and find a chippy shop in Bridgford Road.

'You don't have to do that,' he'd said, quite horrified. 'Mr Nightingale's always got enough over for us. I'll see it's all right for you. You'll have a bite here.'

And from then on, that's how it was. Whenever Mr Nightingale, or Mr Bingham after him, needed a hand with his unloading or any other little job, we would be there to help him. In return, we were given whatever was spare on the menu for the day.

In the year I came to Trent Bridge the cricket table had undergone a major overhaul. Its reputation as a 'featherbed', a batsman's paradise, was becoming an uncomfortable one to support. Bowlers, in particular, never tired of making it the target for their complaints though it was a batsman, Reg Simpson, who in his captain's report for 1952, wrote:

'I am sure the decision to alter our wicket will be for the good of Notts cricket generally. Bowlers must receive some sort of encouragement and they like to see the ball do something off the pitch occasionally as a result of their endeavours. There is no doubt whatever that the wicket during the last few years has been far too good for three-day cricket. However, the playing area has now been treated (or at least two-thirds of it) and everyone is anxiously waiting to see the results. Our one hope, of course, is that it will not go to the other extreme, resulting in the type of wickets they had at Bristol in 1947 and at Old Trafford in 1950, because I am certain that spectators, although they tire of watching batsmen continually in the ascendancy, would become just as tired watching wickets falling rapidly where the batsmen clearly have no chance whatsoever to play correctly. This would result in stroke play as we know it falling by the wayside.'

So, for me, the New Year soon meant plenty of work helping to finish the re-making of the square. Before anything at all had been done to it the committee had sought the advice of several expert groundsmen. There was no agreement on the precise nature of the treatment that would be necessary but they all pointed to the high percentage of marl in the soil, caked solid over the years, as the basic cause of the trouble.

As Eddie Marshall reported in the club handbook,

W.H. Bowles, the groundsman of Eton College, supervised the operation which, to start with, entailed the removal of one inch of the top soil, followed by re-dressing and re-seeding.

Unfortunately, although the new grass had grown quite well and graphs had been kept recording when and for how long the pitches were rolled, watered or otherwise treated, the square played almost as easily as before and throughout that season other experiments were tried.

The big roller was used very sparingly. 'Sometimes,' wrote Mr Marshall, 'grass was left on and sometimes shaved close. On two occasions we hired a heavy Corporation roller, but at the end of the season we were not satisfied. The square had not responded to treatment and was no faster. It was then decided that drastic action was necessary. We decided to re-lay completely two wickets, and a start was made immediately after the last match.'

So this time they took off the top soil to a depth of twelve inches, where layers of marl were still thickly caked. As the dug-up areas dried a crack opened up along the whole length of the wicket about three-and-a-half inches down. This signified 'that previous re-turfing had not knitted to the heavily marled subsoil and was obviously giving a cushioning effect, and rolling in dry weather was only aggravating the problem by causing friction between the two layers'.

In the second part of this book I shall be advising on the proper care and management of cricket squares, such advice being directed particularly to small clubs who cannot secure the services of a groundsman, or perhaps cannot afford one, and the situation at Trent Bridge some thirty years ago is pertinent to their problems. When a club table is giving trouble it is often because season after season too much marl has been larded on to the table, building up into wickets unresponsive to bounce – in other words, 'dead' strips. And in that case the only solution is to dig up the topsoil to some depth and completely re-lay, though of course not before an expert has been consulted for it is an expensive operation.

As the winter of 1952–3 passed and we had the first

glimpses of the spring of Coronation Year I was at last face-to-face with the remodelling of the Trent Bridge wicket and it entailed the kind of work I really like: the nurture of grass – for those delicate blades are all-important to good cricket.

# 6

# DIGGING IN

Winnie and I had a council house in the Aspley estate which had been developed north of the city in the 1920s. We were married when I was on leave in 1942 and she had put us on the waiting list for a council house then. And when I was demobbed on medical grounds in 1944, there it was, at last a place to live where, as a family on our own terms, we could have our own tilt at fortune.

In the morning I would walk over the Trent and into the cricket ground with a light step. All cricket-lovers will know how I felt. If this was work, then what was pleasure? In a few months' time the Aussies would be here, due to meet the county side in a two-day match – shortened by one day so that our visitors could get back to London for the Coronation festivities.

Just a few days later, on the eleventh of June, they would be returning to meet England in the first Test. And I would be at least partly responsible for preparing the strips they would play on.

With the winter gloom lifting and more hours of daylight the acres of fresh green grass positively cried out for treatment. Such tasks as cleaning out the pavilion and the ladies' lockers and mending the outdoor nets were over. Now it was down to the real work of ground management with a vengeance.

We were deep digging and re-laying four wickets a year. One of the biggest problems had been where we would get soil that was suitable to replace the caked marl we were excavating. Fortunately, the Eton College authorities came to our aid. They were laying a new running track at Agar's Plough and offered us the soil which had been removed. Analysis proved that it was exactly the kind we needed. Eton supplied it without charge and our committee had got us a fifteen hundredweight Army truck to deal with it at our end.

First, we had to riddle it to a fine tilth. And we did this on a large barrel-type riddle with a quarter-inch mesh. But it took three men to operate it, one shovelling the earth in at one end and a man on each side turning a handle which rotated the container.

Eddie Marshall saw us at it one morning and immediately came up with a suggestion. Why not connect the handle shaft to the motor roller? That would quicken the process and at the same time release two of our chaps for work on the pitch.

The roller was jacked up and one of the ground staff, who was something of an engineer, soon put Mr Marshall's idea into practice. It was a real time-saver and important to the whole re-laying operation which was lengthy in any case.

After the soil had been shovelled on to the truck it was brought out to Frank Dalling and me in the middle. We spread it layer by layer, two inches deep and on one wicket at a time. This had to be trodden down and lightly rolled, then another layer of earth, more treading and rolling, and the heavy roller to finish. But of course we had to allow the new earth to settle in and so it was about four weeks before we could do the final rolling.

Having pegged out the top, with strings to check the level, we were now ready to lay the carpet!

There was no question of getting the 300 or 400 square yards of turf we needed from an outside source. It might have been a different quality and texture and certainly a different colour.

Any part of the perfect Trent Bridge outfield could have met our requirements but in fact Frank and Mr Marshall had decided to take it from the area in front of the press-box on the Radcliffe Road side opposite the pavilion. As a replacement we partly re-seeded, partly used turves supplied by a member who had a farm a few miles away. It was excellent grass but I believe you can still distinguish it from the rest of the outfield, which bears out my point that grass is not only green but many shades of green.

What surprised me at the time and may be news to most people is that the central wicket used for Test matches could not be included in all this ground renovation, since the MCC, not the Nottinghamshire County Cricket Club, has authority over it. While a Test match is being played at Trent Bridge (and the same goes for Lord's and the other Test grounds) no officer of the club has any right to stroll out and inspect the wicket. Not even the county captain, should he be present.

What would foreigners make of that, I wonder. They are puzzled enough about the game itself. My collaborator has told me that when he was introducing cricket to a French family on the gravel drive of an old presbytery in Normandy he pointed out that an over consisted of six balls. The head of the family was delighted as he had thought to bring along a box of half-a-dozen tennis balls which, as the self-appointed bowler, he proceeded to bowl to the surprised Englishman one by one.

The atmosphere at Trent Bridge, and I was to find the same at Lord's, was relaxed and good-humoured.

Take our annual outing.

At the turnstiles the gatesmen were allowed to have collection boxes for this do. Harry Dalling, the ground superintendent and Frank's brother, was in charge of the funds. 'Well, Mr Dalling,' one of the men would ask, 'how are we doing then? Any chance of Bermuda or Majorca this year?'

Harry would shrug gloomily.

'Prospects aren't good,' he'd say, 'more like an evening on the beer round at the Fox. No, they're not dibbing up these days. Customers can't like the look of your faces.'

Everyone enjoyed this kind of talk. The gatesmen knew full well that in August, on a day when there was nothing on at the Bridge, Nottingham Forest's team coach would come around – the football and cricket clubs were very matey – and off they'd go to Skegness or Maplethorpe or maybe even Rhyl on the Welsh coast.

It was more or less accepted that although the collection was made specifically for the gatesmen, a good many others would be invited on the trip, including Frank, Ron and myself. For when the collection was counted up Harry Dalling would report to the committee and they would always bump up the total so that we could all have a right good day out. Each of us was even given thirty bob 'pocket money' which, I suppose, would represent at least ten quid today.

I remember one year when the coach stood at the ready behind the stands as Eddie Marshall was driven up in his Rolls. He got out and looked at us in amazement.

'Here, what's all this? No work today? Where are you all going?'

It was the outing, we reminded him – the annual do.

'Well I never, you're a lucky lot of chaps,' he said. 'Here I am, just dropped in to see all the fine work you're doing and what do I find – this!' gesturing to the coach, fast filling up with panicky staff, some of whom were half wondering whether they would be ordered out again.

He stood frowning and then, as if he had suddenly come to a decision, shouted: 'All right – to the blazes with work! I'm not going to work my heart out in the office while you idlers are enjoying yourselves. Make room!'

It was a great performance. Most of us well knew that a seat was already reserved for him – and for Mr Poulton who stood by wearing a broad smile. What everybody didn't know was that every year without fail Eddie Marshall personally sponsored the trip, though it became evident once we were on our way.

Whenever we stopped at a hotel or a pub (ostensibly to allow the passengers to relieve themselves) and began to dig in our pockets to get the drinks, we would always find that the round had been paid for.

On arrival at the seaside, and making use of all the fun and games in the amusement park, again the money for the dodgem cars or 'rolling the penny' or making the highest score at hoopla or darts would mysteriously have been supplied.

Then there was the Christmas sensation.

One December, some years after I had joined the ground staff, I was walking over the bridge when a man I often passed on my way to work and who might well have been a county member since he seemed to know me, stopped and said, 'You'll have a surprise when you get in there today. Unless you planted it . . .' He laughed and walked on before I could question him.

As I reached the other side of the bridge I understood. Visible even from there and seemingly rising out of the playing area was a dark green tree. It had certainly never been there before.

However, I was not really surprised to find Eddie Marshall among those standing in front of the pavilion.

'What, in heaven's name, is going on here?' he was saying. 'I know it's the close season but at any time the finest cricket ground in the whole country is no place to grow a damned great tree!'

I joined the group gazing half stupefied, half amused at the sixteen-foot conifer planted just off the precious table.

'Come on then!' roared our chairman, 'let's get it up and out of here.'

But of course that was not his object in getting us out to the middle. The tall spruce was loaded with brightly wrapped gifts, one for every member of the Trent Bridge staff. Mine was carded: To Big Jim – happy Christmas.

I have never met anyone quite so bubbling with generosity and yet so committed to every cause he undertook as Eddie Marshall. The last time I saw him was in 1968, just after I had been taken on as Ted Swannell's successor at Lord's. He called in with Gary Sobers whom he had just picked up off a plane at Heathrow. 'This is the fellow we need,' he told me. '*He'll* put us back on top again. Best all-rounder in the world.'

He was never to know just how Gary revived Nottinghamshire, for he died soon after. And perhaps it was in key with his whole life, for all he did for cricket and our county club, that his last moment came at a committee meeting.

# 7

# IN AND AROUND THE FAMOUS SCOREBOARD

Normally, death does not feature largely in a youngster's life, except perhaps as something glorious like dying for one's friends or one's country – and a taste of real warfare soon cuts that down to size. It may have to be done but there isn't much glory attached to it.

However, thinking of Eddie Marshall and how much I still miss him brings back a strange circumstance connected with the death of my father.

It happened on a day in late February 1936.

I was seventeen and working at the saw mill in Traffic Street. When the siren went I hurried off home for lunch as usual. I remember thinking that I would have to save harder and get myself a bike for the cold and rain were sweeping right through me. At least with wheels I wouldn't have to be out in it so long. Keeping close to the tall grey walls of the warehouses and offices didn't help much either. It had been raining for days and little waterfalls were coming off the roofs and windowsills.

But at last I turned into White Cow Yard where we lived and ducked into the house.

My mother had already got there and the parlour was nice and warm because our good neighbour Harriet had been in, stoked up the fire and put the stewpan on.

'Any news of Dad?' I asked as Mother busied with serving out the meal.

She shook her head.

He had been in the city hospital for some weeks now. I'd

been to see him a few times and of course Mother visited him whenever she could get away from work. We sat down and had started to eat when she said, 'Oh, Jimmy, you've forgotten to wind the clock.'

I looked up and saw that the hands stood at a quarter to eleven though it was well past noon. But one thing I knew for certain. That big impressive clock, set in its heavy ornamented oak case over the sideboard, had been wound regularly. Each time I had been to the hospital Dad had impressed upon me that it was the most important task with which he could entrust me. 'Take care of it, lad,' he'd say, 'it's been in the family for years – and never lets us down once. Give it twelve turns with the key, just twelve, no more, no less. Every Thursday now. Don't forget.'

And of course I hadn't forgotten. It obviously meant so much to him.

Mother was still mithering on about it. 'You didn't touch the pendulum, Jim, did you, but you did wind it up on Thursday? You know how it worries him.'

A little later, when we were having a cup of tea, there was a knock at the door. As soon as I opened it I knew something was going to hit us. The man who stood there was dressed in a rough suit of hospital grey that was too large for him, the trousers all slopping wet over his black boots. In those days, with no social security, down-and-outs with no family were taken on by the hospital, given this kind of uniform and earned their keep by doing odd jobs which included going on errands.

'The superintendent says, give you this.' He thrust a letter in my hand while looking down at his boots.

Mother had got up from the table and I passed her the note, and although she must have known what was in it, she said quite calmly to the man on the doorstep, 'You'll come in and sup some tea?'

The man mumbled a thank-you but said he'd got to get back, so Mother gave him sixpence, closed the door and read the message.

'He's gone, Jimmy,' she said at last. 'They say he died at quarter to eleven.'

There wasn't much more to it. They brought Dad home and set the coffin on a trestle in the parlour. He was all in white and laced up. Mother had been resolutely saving with Pearl Assurance for an eventuality like this. Friends and neighbours came in to see him and everyone seemed to drink a lot. Jack Matthews, who kept the Nottingham Castle pub just across the yard, had worked with Dad in America and no doubt he was the one who made sure the beer flowed.

We could never get that clock to go again and I still wonder about it. Well, it was very strange, wasn't it?

Older cricketers will remember that 1953 was not one of our best summers in terms of weather. But an Australian tour always peps things up and once we had finished the deep digging and re-laying and were occupied with the more normal tasks of fertilizing, spiking, mowing and rolling, the actual season seemed to be right on top of us, even in mid-April. Of course this feeling was heightened by all the activity in the nets and the fielding practice which was all quite new to me.

What I felt each morning as I stood taking my first look at the expanse is precisely what I still feel when I leave my house at Lord's after breakfast and inspect the twin grounds there. A surge of sheer pleasure. The grass all around is so short and yet so lush. Maintaining it in that state is another matter: it entails ceaseless care and patience and a willingness to keep abreast of modern techniques in ground management.

All the same, there is a lot to be said for some of the older methods.

For instance, I am often asked how we prevent any yellowing of the grass, something which is present in many a garden lawn. Apart from spiking and pricking (done in our case by tractor over the large areas of outfield though forks are still used on the table) which aerates the soil and allows water to get right down to the grass roots, I have always relied heavily on caning or brushing. Sometimes it is called 'tipping' because it is a gentle process.

Yellow or light brown patches can be due to various causes but the most common one is fuserium disease. Fuserium has a preference for attacking only the finest grasses, like those on bowling or golf greens as well as on cricket tables, but it cannot flourish if the blades are regularly disturbed.

On a golf course you will often see the greenkeeper swishing his twenty-five-foot cane over the turf, which is what I used to do at Lenton Park, particularly on the bowling green. But at Trent Bridge we used six heads of stiff broom nailed to a long board. The best time to brush is in the morning while the dew is still on the grass.

All the rough weather during the summer of 1953 made our work extremely difficult. While the rain was coming down during a match our main task was to keep the water off the table, taking as much care of the bowlers' ends as the track itself. Mopping up in those days was done mainly with foam rubber mats about a yard wide and six to eight feet long. We would walk on them or use the light roller. The mats would be put through a mangle to squeeze out all moisture and then the process repeated again and again.

As you can appreciate, what is utterly dispiriting is when you have preserved the wicket in fair condition and dealt with the worst parts of the outfield, ready for a re-start, and then another shower breaks over the ground just as you have rolled the covers off!

It happened to us constantly in that Coronation Year.

Although the ground was still soft and in a county championship game our bowlers had skittled out Worcestershire for 70, the early hours of Thursday, June 11th were pleasant enough: we were even promised some sunshine. But when we were marking out the pitch Frank nodded towards Parr's Tree and the hills we could just see beyond. Neither of us said anything. Out there to the east it didn't look at all good. At Lord's it is the westerlies – low leaden clouds drifting in over the visitors' dressing room and the Warner Stand – that we most fear; but at the Bridge it was dense weather coming in over the low country that usually gave us rain – or worse. But at least I could get renewed pleasure from Frank's immaculate lines. He taught me to mark out the batting, bowling and return creases in whitewash lines just half an inch wide. He used to send out for a special fine-tipped brush with which to do it.

Before that, of course, the wicket had to be given its final trim. Frank, as head groundsman, was in charge of the mower. The same machine was always used for this important cut and for the duration of the match the blades were permanently at the required setting. Either Dai Davies or Harold Elliott, the Test match umpires, would oversee the operation. They reported at the ground about nine-fifteen and would expect us to be out there in the middle ready for the cutting and rolling.

My part of it was to drive the roller that yielded the kind of immaculate strip we hoped both batsmen and bowlers would approve. What a hope! In all cricket – not only in Test matches – if the batting side flourish the wicket is deemed to have fair bounce with the ball coming nicely on to the bat, while if wickets tumble it isn't the batsmen's fault but a demon track giving uneven bounce!

It was nearly always the heavy roller we were asked to use. 'Break it up, for God's sake' was the typical remark, based on our reputation for nursing a featherbed.

In this final cutting Frank was permitted to cut just one breed down and another one back. It was the umpire's duty to see that rule was followed. Just five or six minutes and then the roller was on, if wanted.

It was only ten or twelve minutes after start of play that Len Hutton, England's first professional captain, was actually smiling. Alec Bedser swung the first ball of his second over clean through Hole's forward defensive stroke and hit middle stump. Australia 2 for one! And as I watched this wicket fall from our giant scoreboard I had a definite feeling that whatever the weather had in store for us, it was still going to be a great match. Thirty thousand people yelling their heads off might have contributed to that feeling.

But after such a heady dismissal there wasn't much to cheer about – not from our point of view. Morris and Hassett were the kind of gritty batsmen England are always looking for –

the kind that we needed so desperately in the ill-fated tour of the West Indies in 1980–1, the kind who can abstain from dangerous hooking and top edges through the slips, in other words experienced top-class players who can stop the rot. Dull cricket, perhaps, for the casual and uninitiated spectator but certainly not for those who appreciate the absolute necessity to pull a side together after an early shock.

The Australians had taken the score to 54 when a haze of rain sent everyone scurrying to the pavilion for a premature lunch-break.

Drizzle continued to bedevil play afterwards and the pulpy ball must have made it very difficult for the bowlers to swing or spin effectively.

So we pinned our hopes on Bedser – and not in vain. Eventually he nabbed Morris leg-before and had Harvey caught by Denis Compton at fine-leg. Three for 26 and nearly half his 25 overs had been maidens. Nevertheless, in such a murky light the visitors had done very well to put up the 150.

For us, the ground staff, it had been a working day and no mistake. Covers on, covers off; on again, off again. For me, when they were off it was a scamper back to the scoreboard to pick up my duties there.

Bedser and Bailey shared the new ball and before three o'clock Australia were back in the pavilion one short of 250, Alec having taken seven for 55, Bailey two for 75. Godfrey Evans was superb behind the stumps. He took two catches and gave away only four extras.

Now it was England's turn. Our line-up looked formidable with Don Kenyon, the fast-scoring Worcestershire opener, partnering Hutton, our own skipper at No. 3 and after Compton and Graveney, Peter May at No. 6. Who wouldn't give his last tenpenny piece for such massive run-getters today! And, as a stiffener at No. 7 – Trevor Bailey.

Yet when, once again, bad light curtailed play we had lost all but the Essex all-rounder. Thirteen Test wickets in one day! Len Hutton, with 43, was England's highest scorer, Simpson and Compton having joined Harvey, Tallon, Lindwall and Hill on ducks, which made Hassett's 115 shine as bright as a summer's day we weren't getting.

Naturally enough, the ground was packed again on Saturday. The Nottingham air was thick with cricket talk. Would the England tail wag? We still had Bailey and Wardle who should be able to slam a few. But mainly what everyone was asking was, 'Can Bedser do it again?'

The sky was heavy on us, the ground damp but apart from a successful appeal against the light and a short break after tea, the day stayed dry.

The answer to that question came in the sensational collapse of Australia in their second innings. Bedser dismissed Hole, Hassett, Harvey, Miller, Benaud, Lindwall and Hill with deceptive swing, leg-cutters and a generally magnificent show of intelligent pace bowling. Tattersall cleaned up the other three wickets and also took two catches off Bedser. The grass had dried out enough to help his tweakers.

So with the 'old enemy' out for 123, England had the match firmly in their grasp. But there, in our imaginations, the wished-for climax was to stay. Our special local delight was to watch Reg Simpson in an undefeated second-wicket partnership of 94 with Len Hutton – and that took place on the following Tuesday afternoon.

It rained and rained all Sunday and Monday and was still at it on the morning of Tuesday, the final day of the match. There is a photograph of a disconsolate group watching Frank and me treading down those hard-worked foam mats out in the middle of a practically deserted Trent Bridge. The group included Test selectors Leslie Ames and R.E.S. Wyatt, Rex Alston, the BBC commentator – and Bill Johnston, the Australian bowler and their No. 11.

Bill won renown that 1953 season. He topped the Australian batting in all matches with an average of 102. He was not out in all but one of his 17 innings!

The only part that I can claim is having built up on our scoreboard his bowling figures for the Test match: 18 overs, 7 maidens, 22 runs, 0 wickets in the first innings, 18 overs

9 maidens, 14 runs, 0 wicket in the second . . . No doubt it was rather more enjoyable for Bill to walk back undefeated in both knocks – 0 and 4. Back in Victoria over the last quarter of a century he must have been wined and dined many times for his incredible batting record.

But I want to tell you about Harold Butler. He had soon become a particular friend of mine and I was so sorry for him during the 1953 season. Summer after summer he had bowled his heart out for Notts and now that things were coming good a wrenched shoulder had kept him out of the side for the last four or five weeks. He could take no active part in the jubilation that was rippling through the team and our supporters in the final run-up to the season. But there was worse to come.

It happened the following season (1954) towards the end of May. We had already beaten Derbyshire, Somerset and Essex and lost only to Middlesex at Lord's. It was our third home match and we were entertaining Sussex.

We had had some rain overnight and were using one of the newly laid strips which may have accounted for the loss of seven of our wickets without touching the hundred. But our number 8, young Jack Kelly, chose just the right time to make his first ton for the club and, considering what had gone before, Notts' 247 was a fair total. Joe Hardstaff, deputising for Reg Simpson, seemed quite pleased with it.

Having helped Frank Dalling to clean up the wicket, I sauntered off towards our giant scoreboard to pick up my duties there.

It was a complicated business. As you looked at the structure, solitary and solid as a rock in the north-east corner of the ground, the names of the players in batting order were set up on the left, except for the two batsmen who were in. Their names and individual scores, together with any extras and team total, were top centre and electrically operated. We had a chap who sat on the bottom deck pressing buttons all day. All the names of the fielding side were on the right with the appropriate figures against those who were bowling. Ron Allsopp dealt with the upper deck, the first seven players: mine were numbers 8, 9, 10 and 11. And the figures for wickets, runs, overs and maidens were slotted in by hand.

The two official scorers sat in regal fashion in a little box jutting out from the main structure.

With Harold opening the bowling from the pavilion end I knew there was no hurry to get there – you never had to put any runs against him early on, even more certainly, I thought, as tall stoical John Langridge was facing. So I was strolling to where an elderly friend of mine (more about him later) who had just driven up and parked his car behind the boundary in front of the concrete stand backing on to Fox Road. Just then what must have been a hard-hit ball rattled against the row of benches.

'That's off Harold,' said my friend as I came up to him. He was still sitting behind the wheel.

'Off Harold,' I repeated rather stupidly as I rested an elbow on the roof of his car.

But he was right. John must have sneaked a single and the ball, heartily struck by D.V. Smith, had already been collected and returned and there was our redoubtable pace man, head lowered, on his thoughtful walk back.

'Must've slipped out of his hand,' I said. We exchanged the usual pleasantries and had begun to discuss the weather, the quality of the opposition and so on when, as we glanced back at the game, we found the ball soaring towards us again. It was nearly a six, and if it had been it would surely have landed on the bonnet of my friend's car. I gathered the ball and tossed it to a fielder.

I was staggered. Two fours off Harold at this early stage – it was unbelievable. 'I'll have to leave you,' I said, making for the scoreboard.

'Nine off Harold already,' called the operator as I got there.

Soon John Langridge was walking, bowled by Harold for three but all of us at the ground that day could sense something was very wrong. And John told me, when I asked him about it the next day, 'You want to know why Harold got me? Because in that first over most of his balls were nowhere near me, he was bowling off line, and I'd never known him do that before. I couldn't work it out.'

With Langridge out and D.V. Smith cutting loose (he notched up 132 in the end) Harold was obviously straining for more and more pace. But as he raced in once again and his arm whipped over, he stumbled and fell into the stumps.

It was his shoulder. Badly wrenched, they said. And it had given him trouble before. He tried to carry on and even went on bowling. But it was no good: he could do nothing.

He was helped off the field by a couple of players – well, almost carried off. Then he was taken straight to hospital.

It was early in the season, we still had a lot of work to do and it was well past seven o'clock when I was making my way to the pavilion and saw one of the attendants on the balcony.

'Any news of poor old Harold?' I called.

'In the dressing room,' he said. 'Just come back. Doesn't look too clever.'

I hurried into the pavilion and up the stairs to the home dressing room. And there was Harold, all alone, sitting on a form with his right arm in a sling. The attendant was quite right. He didn't look too clever at all.

I felt awkward.

'Well, Harold . . . how are you feeling?'

He just sat and looked at me. At last he said, 'I think it's the finish, Jim. My bowling days. Finished.'

And that's how it was. As far as I could gather his arm and shoulder muscles were badly torn and would take a very long time to mend. At his age, and as a fast bowler, Harold just didn't have that time to spare.

He was still sitting there as I left. Thinking perhaps of the hundreds of first-class wickets he had taken, or, more probably, of the many more he would never take in an empty future.

In the 1954 averages you can read the line:

*Also bowled:*

H.J. Butler 7 overs 2 maidens 26 runs 1 wicket.

We decided there was just one thing we could do to make sure Harold would feel he'd set his mark permanently on that Trent Bridge wicket.

The following season he joined us on our autumn and

winter work. We still had some digging up and re-turfing to do.

'Have you still got your old boots in the locker?' we asked him.

He said, yes, he had.

'Go and get them,' we said.

Then we staged a little ceremony. The interment of a loyal bowler's footwear. After all, Harold had spent some of the best years of his life thudding over that square. Now and, we hoped, forever the boots that had served his cause would lie beneath it. Deep down, of course – so you batsmen who are anticipating having to face the Notts attack need not fret. Unless, maybe, you fear that a whiff of Harold's fire and energy may rise up and strike you out.

One never knows.

# 8

# WHAT MONEY CAN'T BUY

As I said in the previous chapter, there is a little more to say about my friend in the little blue car who was witness to Harold Butler's last over. He was there at every home match and we got to know each other quite well – though not quite well enough, as it turned out.

He was in his late fifties or perhaps much older. He certainly looked rather frail and I suppose it was this which made me feel protective towards him.

He called me Jim, I called him John. Week after week, spring, summer and autumn he'd be there, driving up just before the start of play and always parking in exactly the same place. He was very careful with himself. A pint of beer at the lunch interval, never more. And he brought his own packet of sandwiches. I reckoned he lived alone and was probably a retired civil servant, fairly low in the pecking order, existing on a pittance.

I'd often chat with him between my duties. He loved to discuss the game in progress and the potentialities of the younger players. But we kept it to Jim and John and never became too personal. It was like men meeting in a pub. No surnames, no family talk, yet sometimes you're as close as brothers.

But as the 1954 season drew on I felt he needed looking after. That packet of sandwiches and occasionally a quarter of a pound of sweets, fruit drops or jellies, which he would offer me because he knew I'd given up smoking, weren't enough to feed a sparrow.

If it was a chill raw day, and that kind of day is frequent in an English summer, I'd tell him he should get himself a bowl of soup from the canteen and he always thanked me profusely, as if the thought was quite outside his own terms of reference.

He was in the habit of wheezing and after a fit of coughing would mutter, 'A bit of chest trouble – it's the damp – always catches me.' And I would say, 'Why don't you pack up the fags like I did, they're no good to you, you know.' But neither of us believed he would – and he didn't.

It was a particularly wet summer that year and he seemed more and more bronchial each time I saw him.

Eventually, I said, 'Look, John, I don't know how you're placed but couldn't you skip off to the seaside for a couple of weeks. You'd still get your cricket. How about somewhere on the South Coast – Eastbourne, say. You can watch Sussex. You're bound to get a bit of sun and feel better.'

Rather to my surprise, he did just that. On reaching the ground one morning I found a postcard awaiting me. From Eastbourne. It was mild and sunny there, he told me, but he was lonely. He missed Trent Bridge and our chats.

Before the week had passed he was back again and waiting there in his car for my opinion of the weather, its effect on the wicket and a run-down on the Notts cricket he had missed.

I liked his passion for the game and I liked the man himself. He was so completely self-effacing yet strong in his cricket judgments. Indeed, sometimes he had an air of complete authority which really puzzled me because it didn't fit in at all with his well-worn clothes, his thrift or his general helplessness.

I believe it was the following year that the president's room was due for a spring clean. We all took a hand. Mr Poulton, our secretary, deputed me to wash down the walls. 'And the pictures are getting a bit grimy,' he said. 'Give them a good wipe too, will you.'

The room was plastered with framed photographs – of past presidents, secretaries and treasurers, of Notts stalwarts in action, and quite a few oil paintings of men long dead.

I was about to put one of the photographs aside after giving it a good clean-up when I had a shock of recognition. I held it out in front of me and took another long look. At the same moment Mr Poulton came into the room again.

He came up to my shoulder.

'Ha, I see why you're staring at that one. Your car-park crony. But you know who he is, don't you?'

I couldn't say anything. I must have looked very stupid just standing there goggling.

'Well, there it is,' pointing a finger at the little plate. 'John Ashley Player. He's one of our past presidents. But surely you knew . . . .'

John Ashley Player! A member of one of the most powerful families in the city; the big tobacco firm. That pale, chesty, rather needy friend of mine was part of it.

Come May and our opening match, I saw the blue car arrive but couldn't find it in myself to go over and greet John. Stupid, perhaps, but I just had a feeling deep down that he'd made a fool of me. Eventually, of course, I had to go and see him. He sensed my awkwardness and in his diffident way wanted to know if anything was the matter. So I told him.

He was quite taken aback. But surely – what difference did it make? I shrugged it off because it was something I just couldn't explain, something to do with an assumption between men who get along together that it's on an equal basis. The fault of my background – and his? I can't say. But things were never quite the same again. After that, we were merely polite.

Cricket groundsmanship is hard manual work for much of the time, and that time has to be elastic, depending on the needs of the moment, but what is so satisfying is the knowledge that you and your fellow-workers are an essential part of the game. The Test and County Cricket Board make the fixtures, the club committee engage the players and superintend spectator and catering facilities and the rest of it, but unless you, as a member of the ground-staff team, live and breathe the cause of nursing that precious area of turf, all the careful match-making and spectator provision in the world cannot ensure good cricket and the continuing attraction of the first-class game.

While at Trent Bridge I had a hand in preparing wickets for South Africa (three times), Australia, Pakistan and West Indies (twice) and India. Results seemed to prove that the 'feather-bed' accusation could no longer be levelled at us. Of those eleven Tests England won five, South Africa and West Indies one each and four were drawn.

But if any credit is due, it should go down to the memory of Eddie Marshall, and the committee who supported him. That prolonged re-turfing operation really paid off. And, provided the money is there, I would advise any other cricket club, large or small, which has similar trouble with a table caked hard over the years through over-generous application of marl, to do likewise. It is only fair to the grass which cannot enjoy rooting and shooting in a cement trap!

I often used to feel that Trent Bridge could never be the same without Albert Tordoff. He first made his presence felt as a spectator, a loud, cheery voice, broad Yorkshire, encouraging our lads when he thought they needed it. I'm not sure that it always had the desired effect. I've seen one of our batsmen straighten up looking quite dazed and probably wondering why on earth a fellow from the distant dales should be bothering himself with the fate of Nottinghamshire. But that was before any of us really knew him.

It was about the same time as Winnie and I had moved to a house in Wilfred Grove very near the Fox Road end of the ground. And Fox Road was where Albert had taken a large, rambling Victorian house of many rooms. He was a big red-faced man carrying nineteen or twenty stone. Some people didn't take to him. They thought he drew too much attention to himself. But he went down all right with the rest of us.

Undoubtedly one reason for this was because he kept open house and was almost recklessly hospitable. He and his wife took in anyone who wanted lodgings for a day or two and served meals in their large dining-room. Our committee seemed to look on him favourably. Before long they had arranged for us and the secretarial staff to lunch there regularly. At their expense, I might add.

Albert, who always served us himself, provided such rich fare – in typical Yorkshire style – that a few of the staff had to give up going there. It was too much for them at midday.

I was not among them and I thoroughly enjoyed it. 'Big Albert' was such a life-giver. The whole house hummed with activity and whether Albert was laughing over some joke or throatily cajoling us to have second portions of his succulent meat, potatoes and Yorkshire pudding, his presence made you feel on top of the world. After all, isn't that preferable to dragging round a face as long as a coffin?

He also had the knack of getting everybody talking; and since plenty of the Nottingham Forest lads were also his regulars, plus match umpires in season, any youngsters who had come to Trent Bridge for a trial and maybe one or two of the visiting county side who preferred Albert's rather than a hotel, you could depend on a lot of witticisms amid the babble.

Unfortunately, it didn't last. How could it? Generosity and love of keeping his fellowmen in good spirits was not equalled by any business acumen. Albert had to give up his fine house and soon after moving away, he died.

But there are still some of us who will never forget him and every time I am at Trent Bridge I find myself looking beyond the Fox Road stands and thinking how strange it is that a man can make himself so important for a while to a certain community – establish a beneficient empire in a way – and then vanish like the sun behind a cloud.

In quite another way, one of the images that often comes to mind when I am sauntering about Trent Bridge is the sight of one of our committeemen, Mr J.K. Lane, arriving at the ground.

In appearance he was rather like Harry Secombe once was with a large beaming face, ample trunk and short legs. He drove a high-sided, open car – a Lagonda, I think – and the extraordinary thing was that it made him invisible.

We would be working out in the middle and as this long-bonneted vehicle slid into view somebody would always say, 'Here comes JK – I think!' And all eyes would follow it until it came to a halt. It was something of a relief to see that rotund little gentleman actually tumble out.

I spent sixteen happy and productive years at Trent Bridge. I had worked in the timber mill; from my parents I knew all about conditions in the lace trade; I had friends and acquaintances in the big tobacco and chemical works; and in the Services I had rubbed shoulders with men from every walk of life. So I was in a good position to tell whether being on the ground staff of a major county cricket club was a job that would suit me for as long as I remained active – and, just as importantly, whether my work was satisfactory to my employers. After only a year or two I knew my own mind all right and the Nottinghamshire committee gave me every indication that I measured up to their expectations. I'd become one of the family, so to speak, for that was how they saw it at Trent Bridge – and still do, I assure you.

# 9

# AND SO TO LORD'S

My decision to apply for the position of assistant groundsman to the MCC at Lord's, and thus to leave Trent Bridge, was the most difficult I had ever had to make. I think I have made it plain already that the family feeling at the Nottingham ground was very strong and I could not have been happier in my work.

But once a man gets a real grip on his job, and he is young enough to want to make more of himself, the temptation to step out to pastures new is also compulsive.

Frank Dalling was younger than I so I didn't see much prospect in waiting around for him to retire; also our daughter Christine had married and she and her husband John lived in London.

It is natural for a mother to want to keep in close touch with her daughter, to be around when she was needed, and so Winnie had to make frequent trips to the capital by train. And whenever we were all together the discussion always turned on how much easier and more pleasant it would be if I, like John, worked in London.

It was about that time – 1965 or 1966 – that Frank Dalling and I were invited to attend the first-ever meeting of all the county club groundsmen at Lord's. We met and had lunch in the famous dining-room of the old Lord's Tavern.

The authorities were worried about the varying state of wickets throughout the country and had issued a dictum that we should apply ourselves to ensuring, weather permitting, that our wickets were true and fast to favour stroke play on the part of batsmen. This is all very well but it means much use of the heavy roller and tracks almost devoid of grass. The more you shave grass, then put heavier and heavier pressure upon it, the greater the danger of suppressing strong growth and causing disease and grassless patches. This is particularly the case at Lord's, as I was to learn later, because so many matches have to be catered for on a square hardly large enough to accommodate them.

Anyway, it was a fine day and after the meeting I couldn't resist opening the french window and strolling out on the balcony to see the playing surface that had known so many historic matches.

I couldn't believe what I saw. Firstly, I had never seen a first-class cricket ground with such a pronounced slope. When I asked about it afterwards I was told it was a seven-and-a-half foot drop from the Father Time stand down to the Tavern. And my immediate reaction was, 'How on earth can major cricket be played on *this*?'

The ground staff were working on the table and I was also surprised at what they were doing, which was to scatter top dressing over the precious turf. No pegs, no levelling strings. Didn't they realize that the mixture they were scattering might build up on either side of the uneven spots they were trying to get rid of – and create fresh little humps?

Of course I had little knowledge then of the unique problems Ted and his staff had had to face over many years. When I did come up against them it seemed to me that even our excavation and re-turfing exercise at Trent Bridge was child's play in comparison.

I took an immediate liking to Ted Swannell and I believe it was reciprocated. He showed me around the place and must have been thinking very hard, for as we paused on our tour – I seem to remember it was on the path behind the Nursery terraces – he said: 'How about coming to work here, Jim? I'm sure it'd suit you,' and he gave one of his nervous little coughs that were to become so familiar to me when I saw him during his last days at Lord's.

He seemed to be considering very carefully what to say.

'You know, Lord's is a very special place,' he said at last. 'Lord's *is* cricket – people from all over the world come here.

Just to look at it. It's my place, too, but I'm packing up in '69 and I'd like to know I was giving it over to someone I can really trust – someone who's got his heart in the work like I have. And I know enough about what you've done with Frank at the Bridge to say you're that man.

'Forty-three years, that's how long I've been here. Played for the MCC with the ground staff, took a few wickets, hoped to make it for the county. But I always knew what I wanted – and it was this.' His gesture took in the seven acres, the two grounds, the imposing stands, the clock tower, the other buildings. 'Bloody hard work – yes, it's hard all right – but I love it. And you'd love it, too.'

And he added that before very long the post of assistant groundsman would be advertised. He'd be staying for a year to see the new chap right. Then he'd be off. 'Put in for it, Jim. You'll stand a good chance.'

I asked him if there wasn't someone already on the staff who would also be applying – and surely have a better chance than an outsider.

He mentioned a name.

'But I don't want it to go to him,' he said. 'He's not the one to be boss – a proper Jack-the-Lad. No, he's not the one.'

Persuasive and flattering as Ted Swannell had been I don't think I had applied his remarks to myself. It was as if he had been talking about some other person. I was so bound up with Trent Bridge, the routine, the companionship, the ups and downs of team matters, the easygoing and satisfying nature of the place that, basically, the idea of making a move seemed quite outlandish.

But once again my wife was to crystallize the whole situation and help me to recognize that it isn't always the best thing for a man to wriggle down into a cocoon of contentment and never come out and use his wings. All right, so I had done it once – but here was a chance not only to build on what I had learnt but, in meeting a fresh challenge, to get even deeper into the world of cricket. And I knew, even more surely than Winnie, that this was an opportunity which would't come my way again.

I was forty-seven, just the right age and with the right experience to succeed Ted Swannell. But whoever got the job would certainly hold on to it for many years. It was now or never.

Nineteen-sixty-seven was not a good year for Notts. Dear old Norman Hill did his level best to coax the boys into a winning streak but we finished only two from the foot of the championship table and although I think he had been appointed to lead them again the following season, winds of change were wafting about the ground.

Ever since 1963, when the authorities had properly decided that players might also be gentlemen and gentlemen should be allowed to take up the game as a profession, it was becoming more and more obvious that cricket would have to go out into the market-place and attract a larger public. It must pull in people who either couldn't spare time off work to watch three-day championship games or who thought of the summer game as slow and boring in contrast to sports which produced a quick and positive result.

This was necessary both to keep the counties solvent – following Notts' example and later, even more profitably, Warwickshire, most counties had come to lean heavily on their supporters' club schemes – and to pay the players on a scale more in keeping with their standing in the community.

In contrast to professional footballers, first-class cricketers were being very poorly rewarded for their services. Apart from those who made the Test grade and picked up out-of-season money on tours, the average county pro had the choice of seeking some kind of winter employment or going on social security.

The enormous success of the Gillette Cup, started in 1963, after the genial Cavaliers had shown how the best players of yesteryear could deal with one-day cricket, was making the entry of further big sponsorship into the game more likely. And by 1969 we were to see the establishment of Sunday League cricket under the aegis of John Player & Son – Nottingham to the fore again!

I must say that most of us had our doubts about forty-over

cricket for first-class players. Reduced run-ups for the pacemen, a certain degree of slogging demanded of batsmen, were so foreign to the traditions of county cricket.

Gordon Ross, in an editorial to his *Playfair Cricket Annual*, suggested that it might interfere with the championship if a player was injured on the Sunday and was then unable to take any further part in the three-day match which had started on the Saturday. But he didn't agree with those (and they were many) who maintained that the 'pocket' version of the game would mean cricket 'selling its soul to commercialism'. After all, he pointed out, 'the sustained success of the Gillette Cup with the Company allowing MCC an entirely free hand with administration had done nothing but good for the game in very difficult years'. However, he did wonder if the same could be said about 'individual and team awards on a large scale'. His apprehensions were certainly confirmed by the alarming and confusing events of 1977, when Kerry Packer and his millions burst upon us like a bombshell.

All this was well into the future but perhaps in 1967 I too felt the stirrings of cricket moving into a completely new phase which fortified the decision Winnie and I had reached. Well, it was worth a go!

Needless to say, Nottinghamshire did not make it difficult for me. When the time came, and the MCC advertised for an assistant groundsman, they seemed to fully understand why I wanted to apply for the job.

It was in the late autumn that I went up to St John's Wood for my interview. Quite a few others had applied but I was treated warmly by Mr Bailey, then one of the two assistant secretaries of the MCC, Mr Dunbar, whose research into artificial wickets has proved invaluable to cricket clubs everywhere, being the senior. I had another chat afterwards with Ted Swannell, and again he was most encouraging.

I suppose I must be stoical by nature because I didn't give the whole thing much thought over the next month. But then it was New Year's Day, grey and drizzly, and later that week, with the temperature sinking below zero, we had our first fall of snow. But, for us, the month produced a tonic in the form of a letter from Mr Bailey of the Marylebone Cricket Club. I'd got the job. So it was up to St John's Wood again, this time with my wife, to discuss living accommodation.

Ted Swannell had the house and garden close by the east turnstiles in St John's Wood Road and didn't want to move until he actually retired. When we were shown our present house looking out over the Nursery ground, we felt well suited. I was to start at Lord's in February.

My last working day at Trent Bridge was in keeping with all that had gone before.

Earlier in the month Pat Gibson of the *Nottingham Evening Post* had come along with a photographer who had taken a shot of me leaning rather self-consciously over a hand mower and Pat himself had written a lyrical piece about my move. 'Fancy living at Lord's? It's every cricket-lover's dream – and one that is coming true this month for Jim Fairbrother, assistant groundsman at Trent Bridge for the last sixteen years. A house overlooking the Nursery at MCC headquarters goes with the new job he is taking up on February 26 . . .' And everyone around me seemed equally excited on my behalf.

But when it came to making my farewells – after collecting my cards, clearing my locker and attending to all the little things I'd been putting off for 'another day', a day that now didn't exist – I was met with subdued expressions and there was a strange quietness about the whole place.

At lunch-time I hurried to the TBI, which is what we call the Trent Bridge Inn. I thought of old William Clarke and his All England stalwarts, right in the forefront of cricket in his day, and the thousands of happy hours I'd spent with my mates keeping our beautiful ground up to scratch, and my spirits plumbed. To turn my back on it all!

As Eric, the landlord, was pulling my half-pint I came out of my gloom and looked around the bar. Somehow it was different. Where were all the tables and chairs? Then I saw they had been moved into the lounge.

'What's all this for?' I asked Eric. 'Something on?'

He finished topping off the drink, took the money and gave me some change. He was looking affectedly casual.

'Well,' he said at last, moving to the other end of the bar and starting to add extra polish to some glasses, 'if *you* don't know, I'm not going to be the one to tell you.'

That was all I could get out of him but I should have known. Eddie Marshall, of course, was behind it. He must have told our entire staff to keep a low profile during the morning so as not to give me a clue.

I have no more than a hazy memory of the afternoon and evening, but from what I've been told that farewell party in the old Inn was really something!

# 10

# LARGER THAN LIFE

Moving house is a major upset in anyone's life and it was no different for us. I wasn't due to start at Lord's until the last Monday in February but we came up from Nottingham a fortnight before and stayed with Christine and John at Streatham. I made several trips to St John's Wood to measure up the rooms for carpets and curtains and get some idea how our furniture would fit in.

When we actually moved in on the nineteenth we had to wait a day or two for the stuff to arrive as to justify such a long journey the removal firm had to arrange to serve another family to somewhere on the same route.

We had fun camping out in our own new place but I must admit we had forgotten how chilly a bare, uncarpeted house can be. Remember, it was February and the temperature was hovering only just above freezing point.

Still, we had cups of tea and a meal or two with Ted Swannell, who couldn't have been more hospitable, and when the van did arrive we had a merry old time discussing just where everything should go, and then shifting it again.

Lord's was looking much as it does today. The old Tavern had gone and the construction firm was just completing the boxes in the new stand on the site.

For some weeks after I started work it still felt very strange. Trent Bridge is such a homely place. Everyone knew me, from committee members to gatemen, and I missed the cheery 'Hi, Jim' from this or that corner of the ground.

Lord's, like London, is larger than life to anyone from the provinces. For those who attend the ground only on match days, among twenty or thirty thousand others, it is imposing enough. Row upon row of people from grass level up to those high up in the grandstand under Father Time, and the MCC members packing the pavilion like a convention of judges. At the same time it is full of movement and noise, people coming and going (even during overs, I regret to say), raucous laughter and a buzz of talk; and bright colours shouting at you from the terraces and the Mound Stand.

In the chill greyness of a February day it is so very different. The members' bar and the offices show a few lights, otherwise it is dull, empty and huge. Cricket headquarters, the focal point of world cricket . . . only seven acres of it yet looking more like twenty as I straighten up from doing a bit of brushing on the square.

Yes, I have to admit that for some while I felt like a yokel in the grandeur and aloofness of Lord's cricket ground. I was confident enough in what I had to contribute of my own craft but wondered just how I would fit into the whole scene.

Fortunately, I had little time to think about it for suddenly March was upon us. The new indoor practice hall was nearly ready for use but for the Easter coaching classes we were still required to set up and maintain sixteen nets.

Sixteen! At Trent Bridge we would prepare three strips for practice, three at the most, the wickets being cut on the outfield on the Radcliffe Road end. Here sixteen was the minimum, so that besides those on the Nursery ground we had to improvise matting wickets in the staff car park, in the arbours (normally used as a car park for Wellington Place and for private parties in the stretch alongside St John's Wood Road) and even on the concrete passage under the grandstand.

Once the classes were under way I began to realize how much more demanding my job was than it had been at Trent Bridge. Back in Nottingham we could knock off at five or five-thirty, except on match days and rarely did more than a couple of hours work on Sunday; but at Lord's you can go on well past that and there are so many more wickets to look after that, if you are conscientious, Sunday is no rest period.

But what compensated for it was being part of the general

bustle and excitement. Spring in the air brings out every age and class of crickter from hibernation. Among those coaching the lads were Bill Voce, Tommy Spencer and Freddie Price of Middlesex, Hugh Yarnold of Worcestershire, in his fifties but still looking fit for anything, and another wicket-keeper, Eddie Rowe, who had been in the Notts side when I first worked at Trent Bridge.

Indeed, I soon found that I had by no means left Nottingham behind me. Apart from the meeting with Eddie Marshall, who brought along Gary Sobers, his new acquisition, Ron Poulton turned up for a county secretaries' meeting, came to our house for coffee and then invited us to the Clarendon Hotel, where he was staying, for dinner.

Nineteen-sixty-eight was a wet season, the showers being particularly heavy in the London aeea. A harsh christening, you might think but who was I to criticize the whims of the south-east after so many hours spent watching those rain-clouds coming up the Trent?

Freddie Titmus was captaining Middlesex, who were in process of re-building the side. John Murray had lost his England place and John Price, their pace man, was prone to injury, but batsmen Peter Parfitt and Clive Radley looked good and so did Mike Harris but later he left Middlesex for Notts.

The indeterminate weather naturally made our work more difficult for in many ways it was a crucial season, not least because we had the second Test against Australia in June. Ted wanted so much to go out on a rising note but there was still a lot being said and written about the mysterious unpredictability of the Lord's square.

In the report of their annual meeting in May 1967 the MCC had approved the use of sheet covers for the pitch surrounds while commenting that they 'prevented the new growth of grass on worn wicket ends' and could possibly have been responsible 'for an outbreak of fuserium disease on the square, which adversely affected the production of good pitches towards the end of the season. It has been decided that these sheet covers will be used more sparingly in 1967'. And that part of the report concluded with: 'The Head Groundsman and his staff are again congratulated on carrying out their duties so well, often in difficult conditions.'

At Trent Bridge we never used flat sheet covers for the very reason mentioned in that MCC report. And when we use them at Lord's these days it is simply when it rains during a match and we just have to keep the surrounds dry. But I always have them whipped off as soon as possible.

In the preparation of wickets and the re-making of them after they had been played on Ted's methods were very different from mine but I was only his deputy, the new boy, for this year and there was nothing I could do about it. Moreover, I had, and always will have, the greatest respect for him. I told myself, he must know this ground like the back of his hand and it's not for me to make alternative suggestions.

Lord's has its distinct peculiarities, the slope being one of them. New drainage had been installed before I came with pipes laid in a trench 2ft wide and 15in deep parallel to the pavilion rail – and on the square several wickets had been returfed to help the levelling but you only had to lie down on the grass and look across the table to see that a lot more had to be done to it. I shall be dealing with that in the next chapter.

The MCC knew it and so did Ted but I think in that 1968 season we all hoped that by putting in as many hours' work as we could, and following the same careful procedures, by some miracle our pitch would yet again be considered one of the best in the country. After all, that is what had happened the previous year.

When the ball started flying about in one or two of the county matches Ted's usual cheerfulness was shot through with anxiety. He had acquired a nervous little cough which punctuated everything he said. I guessed it was mental strain that produced it and, as it happened, I was right. Naturally I didn't comment on it at the time but just tried to help him in every practical way I could. However, the first time I saw him after his retirement I couldn't help but notice that the cough had gone.

Like any groundsman worth his salt Ted's aim over forty years had been to produce wickets that were fast and true and yet had a bit of life in them for the bowlers but never dangerous to the batsmen. I knew already how it must have pained him when perhaps the weather conditions combined with some as yet unknown devil in that famous table to spoil the balance between bat and ball.

Looking back on that first year I believe that any unsettled feelings I had were not purely personal. It is always a nervous time when the weather is variable as it was that season. Getting used to entirely different working methods was part of it, I must admit. For instance, I was amazed at the amount and weight of rolling we had to do. At Trent Bridge we did only what was strictly necessary to ensure a level playing area, believing that too much use of rollers compacted the surface and discouraged the growth of a strong healthy sward.

But here we were using not only the little 18cwt roller but the Barford 36cwt and more surprising to me, the great Thomas Lord three-tonner still with its horse shafts on and needing fourteen to sixteen of us to pull it by ropes back and forth. Down the slope from the grandstand to the Tavern we had to be mighty careful and there was always the thought at the back of my mind that someone might slip and be under the monster before we could drag him out of its path.

It is still with us, bearing its name-plate from the old steam engine, and my bosses like it to be used at least once for pre-season flattening of the whole cricket square. But it is no favourite of mine.

Another contraption we used then was the 'duck'. Its flannelled rollers did mop up water on the outfield but it was clumsy to handle and I never liked putting it over the table. It was inclined to take the surface off the pitch and when that happens, you're in trouble. The trueness goes out of the wicket and the ball can fly all over the place.

Wembley Stadium has the reputation of being one of the best natural playing surfaces for soccer in the country, but international show jumping was staged on the pitch that year.

*We were proud of our scoreboard at Trent Bridge and one of my duties was slotting in the players' names.*

*England* v. *India 1979 after the deluge.* (Above) *private parties in the arbour under water and* (below) *the lake that formed at the Tavern end.* (Opposite above) *the covers were not the complete answer to the problem and* (below) *the ground staff boys are valiantly keeping off the water flowing down from the Father Time stand.*

TOTAL
No5 72 No4
BOWLER & OVERS
123456789011S
QANTAS
Standard Chartered Bank
the great international
BINATONE
BRITAIN'S No.1 IN CLOCK RADIOS
CHS PUBLICITY
CONRAD

TOTAL
BOWLER
OVERS
Television Radio Stereo
CONRAD RITBLAT
FOR EVER

(Opposite) *the bomb scare. Our West Indian spectators behaved magnificently but they wouldn't leave the ground!*

(Above and below) *owing to the anti-apartheid demonstrations because of the projected South African tour of 1970 we had to guard the ground day and night.*

*May 1981 was a wash-out with scarcely a match played but only a few weeks later I was waiting for the signal to set up the stumps.*

*Bernard Flack* (above left), *then Warwickshire's head groundsman, shows us his new all-over cover at Edgbaston. At Lord's we have the problem of the 7½ ft drop from one side of the ground to the other and the balloon covers* (centre) *tended to lift in the breeze and were discarded in favour of the present specially designed covers in four overlapping sections* (bottom).

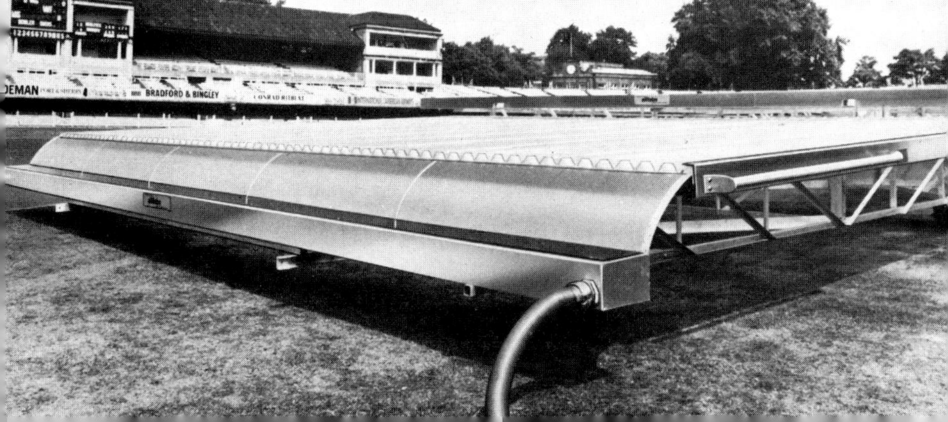

*Presentation to H.M. the Queen 1971.*
(Below left) *H.R.H. Prince Philip presenting the Prudential World Cup to Clive Lloyd, West Indies captain, 1975.*
(Below right) *among the medals presented by Cornhill after the 1980 Test match at Lord's was one for the ground staff.*

*This is how most people think of Lord's during a Test match in the high season but* (below) *is how it was in 1968 – my first season at Lord's – when a hailstorm struck us.*

*With Geoff Boycott* (above) *and Don Wilson* (below) *the M.C.C. coach, in the nets on the Nursery Ground.*

*Installing drains in the mid '60s before I came to Lord's and* (below) *at work on our re-laying operation that took several years.*

(Above) *a Cross Arrows match on the Nursery Ground during September when that club, allied to the M.C.C., plays all its matches.*

(Below) *University hockey occupies Lord's in early summer.*

Our fertilizer supplier, then the head groundsman at Wembley, maintains that the surface has never been the same since so many horses dug their hooves into the precious turf.

Anyway, there was just something about that year of 1968 which produced in me an anxiety I'd never known before. A whiff of ill luck in the air is the only way I can explain it.

The extraordinary curtain-raiser to the eagerly awaited second Test match was the first manifestation of it.

Colin Cowdrey was England's skipper and won the toss, the sun was shining and of course he chose to bat. Australia had held the Ashes since 1959 by winning at Brisbane and Adelaide and twice at Melbourne, the match at Sydney being drawn. But although they had started off this series with a win at Old Trafford there seemed no reason why we shouldn't make it one-all at Lord's. The large crowd was humming with expectation at what batsmen like Cowdrey, John Edrich, Boycott, Milburn, Graveney and Barrington would do to McKenzie, Hawke and Connolly.

But all too soon the sun had been swallowed up by big angry clouds, Edrich was out caught by Cowper off McKenzie and although Colin Milburn had delivered one or two samples of his mighty hooking and Boycott was also pushing the score along nicely, it was obvious to those of us waiting by the sight-screen and constantly glancing upwards that we'd be rushing out the covers any moment.

Coming up to lunch, hard drops began to fall. And, as I said in an early chapter, it wasn't only rain that fell. We knew it couldn't be snow because the drops that hit us as we busied with the covers and run-away hoses stung our faces quite sharply. But when the downpour and the hailstorm passed we could scarcely believe our eyes. The whole ground was a carpet of white. We might have been on the steppes of Siberia.

As the hail melted, first rivulets, then a wash of water poured towards the Tavern rails. As we contemplated it and then tried to do something about it, we must have looked wet, stupid and helpless – because that was exactly how we felt. What on earth can you do about rain and hail in June?

By working unremittingly we did manage to sop up enough

water for play to resume the next day and I kept thinking of how that match went when I was following England's fantastic victories over the Aussies at Headingley and Edgbaston in the 1981 series. For one very good reason. These days we seem to assume that no Australian eleven can be dismissed for a low score. Yet in 1968 England, having made 351, which included Milburn's gloriously punchy 83, Boycott's near 50, and Ken Barrington's workmanlike 75, scuttled out Australia for 78 – and in the follow-on they were only 127 for four when the weather called it a draw.

The wicket certainly played its part and the Aussies were characteristically blunt in telling us what they thought about it. The ball did pop and fly nastily at times but it happened as much for the Australian pace bowlers as for ours. I know Colin was bruised all over because I saw the bruises for myself, and poor old Ken, among others, displayed badly bruised knuckles.

I had been given my full share of preparing the wickets for that season and was as sorry as anybody that the Test trip had caused batsmen such discomfort; but when there is something basically wrong with a table, neither the mower, the roller, the spiker or any other tools or machines can put it right. Much more drastic treatment is needed.

And that is what my next chapter is all about. That notorious ridge, among other things.

# 11

# THAT NOTORIOUS RIDGE

At Lord's we had our very own problem in 1968 and it was hardly a new one. The bumps and bruises suffered by batsmen in the Test match in June were cited by the English and Australian press as clear evidence that the Lord's 'ridge' was no better than it was in '63 when Colin Cowdrey's wrist was fractured by a bouncer from Wes Hall.

All kinds of solutions were put forward, including pitching the wickets from the grandstand to the Tavern instead of from the pavilion to the Nursery end, and digging up the whole square.

The problems of our table no doubt date back to 1814 when Thomas Lord, rather wearily I should think, lifted his turf yet again and brought it here. To accommodate the actual sporting lords of his time he had started on a field where Dorset Square stands now, then moved further north to a site which, four years later, would have had the waters of the Regent's Canal adding variety to the underarm bullets and lobs of the bowlers' armoury.

From the paintings and engravings of the present ground that can be seen in the Memorial Gallery the slope is not very apparent but I am sure it must have existed. And the wickets must have been much rougher than they were depicted. Even in the great Doctor's day batsmen are said to have brushed small stones off the pitch. At least we have got rid of those.

Because of its eminence as the headquarters of the game Lord's has always made the headlines whenever something has happened to its playing area. In the '30s nearly all of its turf was sucked dry by leatherjackets, a disaster which so haunted

Ted Swannell that when I joined he still spoke of it as if it had happened the week before. From what others have told me he dealt with it very swiftly and efficiently and in those days it could have happpened to any groundsman.

Leatherjackets are the larvae of the crane-fly and they feed on the grass roots. As a result the grass withers and a cricket field can suddenly look like a desert. The pests are active in the spring and late summer but the presence of the grubs can easily be spotted and nowadays we have chlordane to put an end to them before they can go into business.

Nineteen-seventy-five and '76 were very hot summers – '76 particularly. Even without leatherjackets our turf was beginning to look brown and tatty. We were still watering the square and some people in the flats overlooking the ground protested strongly to the secretary but Lord's isn't part of the Establishment for nothing!

However, more than one MCC member on returning from his July/August vacation sought me out to ask how on earth we had recovered the playing area from its parched appearance. I said it was no miracle. Because we make sure of strong root growth it is amazing how quickly the blades shoot up after a shower or two. A little mowing and rolling to produce the well-known Lord's breeds – the light and dark stripes – and the eight or nine weeks without rain might never have been.

Presumably that famous Middlesex and England batsman Patsy Hendren wouldn't have donned protective headgear on one memorable occasion unless there had been something in the charge that the Lord's square had its devil. What is so often forgotten in the bursts of Press criticism on this account is that many hundreds of first-class pitches prepared on our table have produced outstanding batting performances and no injuries.

All the same, I knew from my own first year in preparing the wickets that the table was not as level as the one I had worked on for sixteen years at Trent Bridge.

So far as the authorities were concerned, it was not until the Pitches and Grounds Committee was formed in 1967, and reports were submitted by both captains and umpires, that it became obvious to them something drastic in ground renovation was badly needed. So many of the reports spoke of uneven bounce, with the ball coming through at varying heights and making good stroke play difficult.

On my appointment as head groundsman I was left with the legacy not only of these captains' and umpires' views but also an adverse report on our pitches by the county grounds inspector, Bert Lock of the Oval. After careful inspections he had told the MCC that the problem of the ball going through at varying heights could not be solved until some major operation on the square had been carried out.

With Mr Lock and a member of the ground committee present, my staff and I tested various parts of the table. And we found some of them well out of true. In these the pitch of the ball was a good three inches higher than where the stumps were pitched – three inches in five yards, that is.

Over a couple of years we endeavoured to improve the levels by culture operations, by building up the lower areas with top dressings. We were well aware that we could never correct levels which were so far out of true with this method but something had to be done and in this period our pitches were marked in captains' and umpires' reports as 'fast', which meant that the ball was coming through truly enough for batsmen to make strokes.

In the '69 Test series, for instance, the West Indies scored 380 and 295 for nine, England 344 and 295 for seven – over 1,300 runs in all.

The really big operation was still to come and at a MCC Grounds and Fixtures sub-committee meeting, which Bert Lock and myself were requested to attend, it was decided that the square should be levelled over a period of four years, commencing in the autumn of 1972.

We were to work on the basis of treating the 186 x 132ft square quarter by quarter and on the assumption that each levelled section would be suitable for play the second season after the work had been carried out.

Our 118ft sightscreen at the Nursery end played its part in the match programming. For example, it was decided that in 1973 all first-class and county one-day matches could be played in the sightscreen area, whereas in the following years the planning went something like this:

> *Reduced sightscreen area for:*
> 2 Test matches
> 2 One-day Cup finals
> 12 Three-day matches
> *Outside area (top and bottom of square) for:*
> 2 Three-day matches
> 8 One-day John Player League matches
> 2 One-day League Cup zonal matches
> 2 One-day Middlesex 'home' knock-out matches
> *Bottom section of the square for:*
> The Eton and Harrow match (two days); two other one-day schools matches; three Services matches.

I told the Committee that I believed a single pitch should be capable of taking either two three-day matches or one three-day match and two one-day matches.

Before anything was done the MCC engaged a surveyor to square out the area and check the levels. Only when he had sited the main levels – the corners and four intermediate points – could the exact nature of the problem be seen.

Not only were the levels bad from wicket to wicket but across the table it was slightly hollowed; a hollow not a ridge.

So we had a choice. Either we could take the whole of the top off, to a depth of eight to ten inches, possibly more, or take just two inches and level *up*.

Because excavation would have meant a lot of extra work with the table taking much longer to settle down Bert Lock and I favoured the levelling up process and this was readily accepted. It meant that our traditional Test wicket, with other middle strips, would be treated by top dressing the low levels but not replaced.

The turf on the rest of the table, however, an area 41 by 76ft, was removed and replaced by turf cut from the Nursery ground, this having received special cultivation in readiness for use. It also took much time and care to marry the outfield to the new square.

Bert Lock's advice all through this was very practical and helpful and afterwards when he dropped in with reports on his visits to other county grounds he would look me up and we'd chat about this and that.

It always worried him when a fellow groundsman found himself in some sort of trouble.

'You see, Jim, he's been let down by his top dressing. Bought the wrong stuff. And there it is, covering three of his best wickets; couldn't get it off; leaves him topless. Nothing wrong with his preparation – nothing at all. Right sound chap, as you know, and I wish I could've helped him more. But there it is . . . there it is.'

And one day, towards the end of the season, he gestured with his thumb. 'I see your table's getting a battering again. I wouldn't have your job, not for all the tea in China. Too frustrating. Too many matches for too small a square. Never mind, boy. Got to get going, I suppose. See you again.'

As usual he had put his finger on it. At Trent Bridge we had nowhere near the number of fixtures that we have to accommodate at Lord's. And Trent Bridge, like the Oval, Old Trafford and many other county grounds, have bigger tables than ours. The number of three-day County Championship matches has been slightly reduced and the John Player League matches on Sundays are no great burden on the square, and some of the minor games are now played elsewhere than Lord's, but we still have to think in terms of something like thirty-five matches a season.

For Ted Swannell it was a real headache because he had to take in more MCC, Services and school matches than we do now, plus representative fixtures like Gentlemen *v.* Players and some fourteen Middlesex games. Marvellous variety, the passing of which many older MCC members must regret, but it is no wonder the square looked like a battlefield in September, as I am told it did.

The run-up to the 1970 season was bizarre. Throughout the autumn and winter of '69 all kinds of discussions had been going on, official and otherwise, as to whether we should receive the South African tourists who were scheduled to visit us.

At the same time Peter Hain and others had organized a 'Stop the Tour' campaign and were threatening to interfere in all sorts of odd ways with any matches the South Africans played over here. Peter Hain himself had declared that although he would direct concerted action to stop play, there would be no violence. Nevertheless, reports soon came through to Lord's of damage being done to county grounds all over the country and the MCC realized that Lord's itself would sooner or later be one of the demonstrators' main targets.

Several hundred reels of Danert (barbed) wire were delivered to us for the protection of the ground at vulnerable points, and to set up round the cricket table. The staff was also asked to operate as volunteer night-guards.

We paired off and I found myself keeping watch with Stephen Green, the curator of the library and the Memorial Gallery.

It was a fairly bitter winter. In mid-February we had a roaring blizzard and in the deeper watches of the night Stephen and I would be sheltering in the Long Room, from which we had a comprehensive view of the whole playing area. And what an extraordinary sight! A snow-clad Lord's, with the light from the arc lamps at each end giving a sparkle to the white carpet and picking out sharp points of the bristling wire. It had the look of a menacing Christmas card.

And there we sat on the big heavy table, dangling our legs, shivering a little but somehow enjoying the sole occupancy of a room normally used only by the privileged MCC members and Royalty.

Of course, we also did our rounds, to see that no one was creeping around the terraces and stands, and I might add that we were not sorry to quit the pavilion after being there for an hour or two. You have no idea how many strange creaks and rustlings the old Victorian building can conjure up in its vast emptiness. I don't think either of us would have been more than mildly surprised if an old cricketer's shape had glided past us to stand gazing at the ermine-coated turf where he had hooked a ball for six or shattered the stumps.

It wasn't until the third week in May that our vigil ended. There was an emergency debate in the Commons on whether the tour should go on and shortly afterwards the authorities decided to call it off.

# 12

# THE GROUNDSMAN'S LOT

Throughout this book I have made frequent references to the importance attached to the making of a wicket that will satisfy match officials, captains, batsmen, bowlers, spectators and the media. The *perfect* wicket? But for whom?

Any man reckoned to be a first-class groundsman will not have reached that grade without discovering that as well as having the basic essentials of his craft he must also possess an equable temperament, a strong nerve when under criticism and a mind open to any technical developments that may help him in his work.

I am very fortunate in being employed by a body that believes in appointing executives who are familiar with every facet of the first-class game. Most of them have excelled as players and then proved that they also have administrative qualities, vision and at the same time a deep regard for the very spirit of cricket – something that in recent years has taken rather a bashing.

Alec Bedser, who served the Test and County Cricket Board so long and so faithfully over a number of years, touched on this when Peter West interviewed him on BBC television on the eve of his retirement from office.

Mr Bedser said that one of the great things about the game was that however hard it was played on the field, the players always got together in real friendliness afterwards.

'When I was in the England team,' he said, 'and we were playing the Australians down under, we always went to their dressing-room after the match to have a few beers with them. I just hope that spirit will never disappear.'

He went on to say that the pressure on the players had increased over the years. Test series had gone from five to six matches plus one-day internationals. On top of that for our chaps were the regular home competitions – the Schweppes three-day County Championship, the Gillette (now NatWest) Cup, the Benson & Hedges trophy, the Sunday John Player League and all highly competitive.

It all brought more money into the game so that the players were very much better off than their predecessors. And it was right that they should receive what they were worth.

But it was also essential to cricket that it should be played with real enthusiasm and he would like to feel that the youngsters who had its future in their hands were playing it because they enjoyed it.

A match that possibly underlines Mr Bedser's remarks was the Centenary Test at Lord's at the end of August 1980.

The scene was set for a match that would embody the finest elements of cricket. Many great players of the past were there to see it, including many of the party of eighty Australians who had been specially flown over for the match.

In the Melbourne Centenary Test of 1977 that approach to the game had been achieved. After low totals in both first innings Australia had declared at 419 for nine, Rodney Marsh having contributed a century in his best, gloriously uninhibited style to be countered in England's second innings by a similarly free-hitting 174 from Derek Randall. Amid tremendous excitement England failed by just 45 runs to match the Australians. But all those who went over to see the game said that the result (as it happened, the same margin of runs as in the match one hundred years before) was not what they would remember. The best thing about the game was the spirit in which it was fought.

It was not surprising, therefore, that great expectations attended the gathering at Lord's.

To be fair to everyone connected with the game, myself included, the weather was cruel. I am sure this had something to do with the apparent unwillingness of both captains to make a real game of it. Even the hardiest of spirits can be dampened by intermittent rain and baleful skies.

At the outset the wicket we had prepared seemed to meet with approval. Michael Melford in the *Daily Telegraph* said it was 'of an excellence to make the old Test batsmen watching consider a come-back and the old bowlers bless the wisdom of their retirement'. Having watched several overs Mr Melford went further: 'the pitch looked and was soon established as a beauty'. But this was after an infuriating drizzle had delayed the start of play for fifty minutes. Up to that morning we had had at least ten days of scorching sunshine.

Australia went in at the lunch interval with over 50 on the board and not having lost a wicket. By the end of the day they were 227 for two, Wood having reached his century and Kim Hughes on 47.

The next day they lost Wood and Yallop and added fifty but the drizzle hung about, thickened and then it poured. And we had some rain in the night as well.

Late that evening and early on Saturday morning we did everything we could to dry out the outfield. The following day's *News of the World* said: 'Groundsman Jim Fairbrother and his staff were adamant that play could have started on the Saturday before one o'clock, two-and-three-quarters of an hour before it took place.'

That was stretching it a bit. A brilliant sun shone over Lord's and certainly we did consider the ground was playable, and of course the wicket and bowlers' ends were unaffected, being under cover. But it wasn't for me to more than offer my opinion when I was asked – and not by a newspaper!

Perhaps my attitude, as the debate went on around me, showed more plainly than I intended what my own views were.

The outfield, particularly on the Tavern side, to which water runs from the higher ground up by the Father Time stand, was still damp. In some spots the water came up when you pressed your foot down hard, but I'll wager no club cricketer would have hesitated for a moment to be out there on it and getting on with the game. In this case who didn't think play could start – the umpires, the captains? I can't say.

What I do know is that, generally speaking, professional cricketers of today fear possible injury when running sharply or at speed on even slightly damp grass.

My own feelings on that miserable morning were that on such a prestigious, never-to-be-repeated occasion, more willingness on somebody's part might have been expected.

What could not possibly be justified was the behaviour of a few MCC members towards Dickie Bird and David Constant, the umpires, when they returned to the pavilion with captains Greg Chappell and Ian Botham from yet another inspection of the ground conditions.

Impatience was the mood of the morning. The four men were trying to get past the members crowding round them for information when arms were raised, the umpires jostled, someone made to punch David and Dickie was slapped on the back of his head. The captains turned back, rescued the umpires and hurried them into the pavilion. But from what I heard afterwards, abuse was still being hurled at the captains even as they made their way upstairs to the dressing rooms.

Maybe the general ill-will which all of us felt being directed at us by those who had paid good money to see a day's cricket infected the Press Box as well. Far from being 'a beauty' or 'of an excellent, etc' the pitch had become, in Tony Lewis's report on the subsequent play, 'too slow and low for a conclusive Test battle'.

Mr Bailey said, in his statement to the Press: 'Everything that could have been done to dry the ground was done and MCC wanted play to start much sooner than it did. But, in the opinion of the umpires – and in the laws of the game they are in total charge – the ground was not fit to get the game underway any earlier.

'Although the captains accompanied the umpires on their last inspection, they had nothing to do with the final verdict. I was keener than anyone to resume the match earlier.'

On the Monday and Tuesday someone up there took pity on us and produced a clear sky and plenty of sunshine. Chappell and Hughes enjoyed themselves, showing all their strokes, and the captain declared at 189 for four, setting England 370 to win.

Of course it was too much to ask but somehow we all hoped England would throw caution to the winds and have a go.

Geoff Boycott scored a measured 128, Mike Gatting an uncharacteristically sober 51 and stumps were drawn with England still needing 126 runs.

But there was great applause . . . for John Arlott, who had just given his last BBC radio cricket commentary. Poor John. If he had had a choice I am sure he might have picked any of a dozen other matches that would have been nearer to the spirit of the game than this one.

The second Test match of the 1981 series I dealt with in the first chapter. I found it an interesting and evenly balanced game. Perhaps the final phase was rather tame, with England batting slowly and steadily to set Australia a target scarcely within their capabilities in the time left to them. And their loss of four wickets in getting to 90 I thought was a tribute both to their urge to tackle the deficit and to England's bowling. In the first innings a total of 656 runs had been scored and in their second knock England had been well on their way to 300 again.

So I was puzzled that Kim Hughes should be among those who, by the time the Oval Test came round, were saying how imperfect the pitches had been at Trent Bridge, Headingley and Lord's.

In his first knock at Lord's Hughes had made an enterprising 42, getting out to a difficult overhead catch in the deep by Bob Willis. It was in John Emburey's first over of the day which might have accounted for it. In the second innings Graham Dilley got him leg-before-wicket. Neither of the deliveries which caused Hughes's dismissals seemed to have anything to do with the pitch but I could be accused of bias. And I must say that experienced observers were talking of the variable and uneven bounce of the ball by that time.

What a complex subject it is. Naturally, as I was not present at the other two grounds I can offer no comment. But the Trent Bridge match was the only one the visitors won in the series, and Kim has acknowledged that at Headingley it was inspired bowling and catching, with an unpredictably nervous response from the Australian batsmen, that won a madly exciting game for us.

That is no defence for the state of the wicket but at least it made Headingley the theatre for one of the most amazing turnabouts in the history of Test cricket.

In fairness to the Australian captain I should mention that Mr Carr, secretary of the Test and County Cricket Board, told the Press the day before the start of the final Test at the Oval that he accepted or acknowledged Kim's complaints about the 'lack of good batting wickets in this year's Test series'.

Donald Carr went on to say: 'But there was no evil intent on our part or malice on the part of the groundsmen and I don't sense that Kim's criticism was that England was trying to prepare pitches favourable to us.'

He also made the point that at least the pitches had produced results, as distinct from those in some past series which had forced unexciting drawn games.

Could there be an 'ideal' pitch?

He said, 'Some batsmen think it should be flat, slow and comfortable. Some bowlers think it should have pace and bounce and turn a bit at some stage of the match.

'I'm looking forward to asking Kim Hughes his views on the ideal pitch. I'm not criticising him for criticising pitches. But I'd like him to be constructive on what sort of pitch he thinks is ideal, or where they are.'

All I know is that we are not the only country in which surprising things happen.

Our BBC commentators had some really alarming things to say about the state of affairs at the Queens Park ground, Port of Spain, Trinidad on the last day of England's match there against the West Indies.

Apparently, damp spots had appeared on the square when the new, lighter covers were removed. 'The old covers were more effective,' said one commentator, 'because the water lying on the covers was taken by hoses fifty yards away from the pitch.' And Colin Croft, in his run-up from the north end, was said to be 'crossing the swamp that held up play on the first day'. This was due to an 'underground tap' that had been left on.

And play had to start twenty minutes late because the ground staff had not arrived.

Now that is something I cannot ever recall being levelled at the ground staff on any of our Test grounds. For good or ill we are present, on time and ready to receive bouquets or brickbats.

# 13

# A PLACE FOR ALL SEASONS

I never thought when I left Nottingham that I would be able to say, 'I'm going up to London to meet the Queen.' But I had only been at Lord's four years when I was accorded that honour.

On the Monday of the Lord's Test, whoever England may be playing, the teams are presented to Her Majesty if her engagements permit. And it was in 1971 when she particularly asked the MCC if she could also meet members of the staff whom she felt had contributed over the years to the prestige of the occasion.

Ray Illingworth was the England captain and it was the season of the Pakistan/India twin tour.

What I remember very clearly is that I had no prior notice of the Queen's intention. The first I knew about it was when one of the gatemen buttonholed me with a message from secretary Billy Griffith that I was to be presented to the Queen just before the tea interval.

I scurried home to put on my best suit and, having told Alec Gull, my deputy, where I would be, walked round to the pavilion while the last few overs before the tea interval were being bowled.

Among those assembled outside the committee room, were Charles Ray, head of accounts; Audrey Jones, also in accounts – she handles, among other things, MCC members' tickets and has been on the staff practically all her life; Henry Johns, the professional coach for real tennis; the club superintendent 'Young Dick' Gaby and his brother, Joe. The name of Gaby is as renowned in Lord's circles as any cricketer who has ever played there. I believe Dick's father, 'Old Dick', was around the place for something like sixty years.

We did not have long to wait and I was glad of that. I felt pretty nervous. At the best of times I have what is commonly called a ruddy complexion and I could feel it getting redder every minute.

I knew that it would not be proper to say anything unless I was asked. But I couldn't help wondering whether the Queen would just smile and pass on or whether she would actually address me, and somehow I wasn't sure if I would be able to produce a sensible answer.

It had all come upon me so suddenly. Probably Mr Griffith himself had not known of the Queen's wish until the arrival of the Royal party.

I need not have worried. When Mr Griffith introduced me she gave a direct smile and asked how long I had been at Lord's. I said I was a 'new boy', not, as yet, a 'long server'. And I added that I had joined the MCC staff from Trent Bridge.

That seemed to interest her very much.

'Trent Bridge? My father went there several times, and my husband has been there, too. Do you find it very different here? So many games are played at Lord's, aren't they.'

Then she smiled again, most graciously.

'Well, this is London,' she said.

Which I felt, on reflection, said everything.

My meeting with Prince Philip in 1975 was just as precipitate but lasted rather longer.

It was a tremendous occasion – the first Prudential World Cup final, a one-day sixty-over competition which, for the first time ever, had brought teams from seven other countries to join England in a tussle for a new trophy. The sponsors had put some £100,000 into it.

In the first round the countries competed in two groups of four, a system similar to that now used by FIFA to seed out the competitors for the soccer World Cup. We staged England's match against India which our lads won quite easily, with a century from Dennis Amiss and half-centuries from Keith Fletcher and Chris Old, but the rest of the games were spread around the other traditional Test match venues – Edgbaston, Trent Bridge, Old Trafford, Headingley and the Oval, the two last-named also having the semi-finals between the two top countries in each group.

England, who headed their group, lost to Australia by four wickets – all out for 93 with Gary Gilmour taking six for 14. And the West Indies beat New Zealand. So it was Australia and the West Indies who came to Lord's for the final.

We had given the wicket its final cut under the close inspection of the umpires, Dicky Bird and Tom Spencer, and our big 36-cwt machine was ready for its slow rolling up and down the strip, when one of the stewards brought me a message. It was from Mr Bailey.

Prince Philip had arrived to see the match and Mr Bailey would be bringing him out on to the playing area before the game started. Would I assemble my staff so that we could be introduced to the Royal visitor. Prince Philip was always interested in everything that was going on so it wouldn't be just a brief handshake.

And I am sure that also in Mr Bailey's mind was that Prince Philip's appearance on the field would put an authoritative stamp on this new international enterprise and give the finalists an added incentive to make it a really good game.

Most of the people who had been queueing outside the ground were now packing the terraces, the Mound stand and the Tavern enclosure. Even the Father Time stand seemed full. There were still gaps in the members' pavilion seats, the small stand for members' friends, the rovers' benches and in the Warner stand, but we knew these would all be occupied within the hour.

Already the noise was terrific. The West Indian supporters were there in strength and were laughing, waving, whistling, drumming away and hooting.

As Prince Philip and Mr Bailey came out of the shadow of the pavilion, down the steps and through the little white gate there was a moment's suspension of the uproar and then, fortified with clapping and cheering from the non-partisan spectators, rose to a quite deafening pitch.

We were lined up very correctly on the square but the cheery handshakes were soon over and when we broke up Mr Bailey had wandered over to view the outfield, so I conducted Prince Philip to our prepared wicket.

'We've got a glorious day for it,' he said, glancing up at the cloudless sky. 'I have a feeling we're going to see some great cricket here.'

Then he looked up and down the pitch.

'Where's all the grass? None at all on this wicket.'

I assured him that was quite normal. The match strip was always close-cut – shaved. Its brown, polished appearance showed it was just right. The grass was there all right but if we left more of it on it would become a 'green 'un' and the batsmen would be given a hot time.

'But,' said the Prince, 'you realize, don't you, that I'm a fast bowler. If I play here I shall want to play on more grass than this.'

What could I say to that? But he gave me one of those straight, piercing blue looks of his which assured me he was leg-pulling.

As we strolled around the wicket he asked me about Trent Bridge. Like the Queen, years before, he wanted to know if I found it very different here. I said, yes, it was very different.

Then he asked me all manner of questions. What were the processes involved in keeping two playing areas in such perfect condition, how did we decide on what weight of roller to use in varying weather conditions, did we have enough modern equipment, was this my full complement of staff – if not, how many extra chaps did we have to engage for international matches like today's – and so on.

We must have been chatting for ten or fifteen minutes before Mr Bailey came up and gently suggested to the Prince that they had better return to the pavilion if the start was not to be delayed.

Prince Philip said something like, 'Good lord, let's go then,' waved goodbye to us all and strode off.

You don't have to be with Prince Philip for more than a few minutes to know that you have the privilege of speaking to a truly remarkable man. Above all, he makes you feel that your work is worthwhile, that it is somehow unique and of real value to the community. His interest in it is not mere polite interest. He really wants to know. And you have only to ponder on the hundreds, perhaps thousands of people he meets in the course of his Royal duties every year to appreciate how much goodwill and enthusiasm he must disseminate.

The match itself constituted one of the longest days of first-class cricket any of us could recall. The first over was bowled at eleven o'clock in the morning and the 118th at nearly a quarter to nine in the evening.

West Indies were put in to bat by Ian Chappell and, impossible as it seemed on such a sunswept day, in a very short time there was only 50 on the board with three good batsmen gone. Fredericks stepped into his wicket trying to hook a short one from Lillee out of the ground, Kallicharran was caught behind by Rod Marsh fencing to the off in the manner of so many of our England batsmen in recent Test series, and Marsh scooped up another catch to get rid of Greenidge.

But we shouldn't have discounted Clive Lloyd, skipper of his side and as deceptively gangling and goggled as ever. To a tumult of bells, hooters, tin-clattering and shouts he proceeded to lam the bowling to every part of the ground. I found it incredible, watching from the Nursery end, how he could pick up the lightning deliveries of such speed men as Lillee, Thomson and Gilmour and hit them on the rise with the power and accuracy to foil the wide circle of boundary fielders.

With Kanhai he lifted the score to one short of 200 for the fourth wicket. At No. 6 Viv Richards, on his favourite ground, could not even manage double figures but the later batsmen profited from their captain's fine aggressive innings and West Indies wound up with 291.

No West Indian was run out but when Australia batted umpires Dicky Bird and Tom Spencer were soon dashing from behind the stumps to adjudge desperate bats and bodies reaching for safety. Five Australians fell to the swift spot-on throwing of the West Indians – Viv Richards, in particular, enjoying himself. The last run-out of all was possibly the easiest for the fielding side, Thomson lying full-length just short of the popping crease and it was also the culmination of the most extraordinary confusion and hilarious uproar I had ever witnessed at Lord's.

Just before Thomson's dismissal, which gave West Indies the match by 17 runs, he and Lillee had hit and run to great purpose, particularly when overthrows resulted from a no-ball that Thomson had slogged into the hands of Fredericks.

However, with all the yelling, whistling and banging scarcely anyone, apart from the players, had heard the umpire's call. I missed it myself.

The West Indian spectators, the youngest of them already crouching on the boundary line like sprinters, had quickly given Thomson out caught and invaded the pitch *en masse.* The utter confusion had engulfed us all – but there, in the midst of the invading army, were Lillee and Thomson industriously running back and forth accumulating runs. Nobody knew where the ball had gone.

The umpires granted them only three in the end, though it seemed to me that for calmness and perseverance alone they deserved a dozen or so.

And Prince Philip?

He had sent word cancelling any appointments he might have had at Buckingham Palace because, as president of the MCC that year, he had fully intended from the start to present the Prudential Cup and medals to two great teams.

Moreover, he also insisted on making the presentations in front of the pavilion, not from the balcony as was planned. His security men and the local police did not appreciate it at all – the police, particularly, were nervous of trouble on their patch.

But the crowd loved it. And it crowned a magnificent and long day's cricket.

The Nursery end at Lord's could not have been more aptly named – even more so now that we have the indoor playing school. Yet the nature of cricket is such that at any time of the year that end of the ground is by no means the haunt only of youngsters. Sooner or later everyone comes there.

The Cross Arrows cricket club, who traditionally play on the Nursery square every day, bar Sunday, through most of September put out sides that are a fascinating mixture of young and old. Variety stars, band leaders and actors, solicitors, business executives and veteran pros run around in company with MCC's Young Professionals. Their dressing-rooms and balcony are over our mess room and equipment sheds so, in the breaks from work, I see part of most of their games.

Touring sides always have net practice at Lord's and a few seasons ago it was Dennis Lillee and Rod Marsh who swung the usual wisecrack at me when we met on the path round the Nursery ground.

'Hi, Jim. How's the wicket? Doing your worst for us?'

Then there are the dedicated pros one knew so well in the past. One summer, as I was repairing a badly worn net strip, a round-faced genial-looking fellow hailed me and rushed up to shake hands. It was Alan Watkins, one of that fine Glamorgan team that, for the first time ever, won the County Championship in 1948. A left-handed all-rounder, Alan was also a valued member of the England side. He played a bit of football too for Cardiff City and Plymouth Argyle. He was still turning out for his county in 1960 and we'd often had a jar together at Trent Bridge.

He reminded me that we'd last met at a ground management conference in Aberystwyth.

'I'm a groundsman myself now,' he said. 'And I tell you this, boyo. When I was playing I never realized so much work and care and sheer know-how went into preparing a wicket. I'd just walk out there, prod it with my bat, think it was pretty fair but maybe no great shakes – and then *use* it.'

He said he had learnt a lot at the meeting we had attended and had taken a few courses and was now looking after the playing fields at a private school. And he certainly looked very fit and happy on it.

I asked him if he'd seen anything of 'the Big Man', Wilf

Wooller, his skipper in those days. 'Every so often,' Alan said. Wilf would never change. Never said "bloody good innings" when you'd pulled the side round. Never praised anybody. But you knew he'd appreciated it. He always had the boys with him.'

One glorious September morning, with the table and outfield already free of its summer scars and looking rolled and serene – that's how my bosses love to see it – I was sitting with Reggie Moore, my co-author, on a bench under the empty terraces talking over this book, when a man who had made a slow circuit of the playing area paused by the sight-screen. A slight figure, leaning heavily on his stick.

'Jim,' he called. 'You don't mind if I tread your precious turf?'

'Any time, John,' I said. 'Pleasure to see you.'

I knew him, of course. Most mornings I would see him doing his round.

Reggie looked up. 'Good heavens,' he said, 'that's Jack Young. When I think how many times I've sat up there on the terraces watching that left arm wheel over. Using the slope. What a bowler. He certainly did Middlesex proud. Nobody ever leaves Lord's, do they . . .'

'Not if they've got any sense,' I said.

And that's what it's all about. The whole place lives and breathes cricket. It seems to defeat mortality and persuades us that things will go on much the same forever.

Except in the winter, when things naturally ease off and the boys and I have time to clean and service all our equipment, spruce up the place and attend to jobs that could not be done in the season, the activity in and around Lord's could be quite engulfing. After sixteen years I am used to it.

The day's cricket has ended. We have tidied up the wicket, filling in the holes made by the bowlers with our special mixture of soil, grass seed and a doughy substance that dries out hard. Then Alec and I have yet another look at the two or three wickets we are nursing for future games. If the weather is holding fair we leave them to get the evening and morning sun and any breeze, conditions most favourable to grass growth. If the weather forecast threatens rain or one of those icy blasts from the east, then we all have to set to and get the flat covers on.

I might have to discuss the next day's work schedule with Alec, modifying it according to the probable conditions. And of course we always have to think of the two grounds, not just the big match area – seven acres in all. I like to have the whalebone brushes taken over the outfield regularly to whip the dew off the grass blades. For one thing it is a precaution against fuserium which thrives on dampness: for another it promotes a strong cushiony thatch for the fielders.

The scarifying, spiking, mowing and rolling goes on all the time in one quarter or another.

While we were working on the square we will have seen MCC members walking over to the practice nets on the Nursery ground. From the end of April onwards the nets are theirs from five-thirty to seven. As head groundsman I am naturally expected to be around and after the practice the nets have to be closed and roped off. We also do a bit of tidying up for the next day. We are lucky to be done with that before half-past seven or quarter to eight.

Nowadays after the day's play spectators are expected to leave the ground in reasonable time after stumps are drawn but when I first came to Lord's on some nights they were still roaming about at seven or eight. Only when they had all been shepherded out could the gates be shut. A certain amount of pilfering was what induced the MCC to take a slightly less relaxed view of the public.

The Cornhill Test matches and, nowadays, the Prudential one-day games with the touring side, and the finals of the Benson & Hedges and the NatWest competitions put a different complexion on everything connected with my work.

On the day before the match – Wednesday for the Tests – we have both England and the touring side for net practice, England in the morning, and visitors in the afternoon. At three o'clock the Press are invited to inspect the wicket. There is one cricket correspondent on a popular newspaper who delights in pointing out what he will maintain are bald spots or weeds. 'Watch him,' one of the others will say, 'he's got a dandelion all ready in his pocket.'

The England selectors also come along to give it a close look but not at the same time as the Press. They have the square all to themselves.

The BBC television engineers will be busy moving their big crane into position over the sightscreen in the gap between the terraces. I have to be on hand to see to them and to the positioning of the sponsor's and other advertisement boards. And Colonel Stephenson, who has to be all over the place, will spare a moment to tell me, among many other things, how much room we must expect to allow for an overspill of spectators to sit on the grass behind the boundary boards. It can be four or five thousand.

In addition, senior police officers are much in evidence, discussing with MCC officials the usual arrangements for keeping order, including the presence of a plain-clothes squad. These chaps move among the crowd to discourage the activities of pickpockets who work in teams and tend to concentrate on the bars and the paths around the ground where people saunter during the intervals.

Besides their usual duties eight or ten policemen are given the special job of helping me to safeguard the wicket and the square. We have to rush on to the pitch with the ropes at close of play. It is a good idea for those who have supported the match to have the chance of seeing the strip on which it all happened – Colonel Stephenson is certainly in favour of it – but it is essential to prevent the over-eager from trampling over it.

Administratively, any big match at Lord's is very demanding and I think the MCC do a great job. The ticket distribution is done very fairly, smoothly and efficiently; a steward is appointed for each group of seats, several to each block; there are patrolmen for the spectators seated on the grass; we have extra gatemen; and the caterers of course have to take on many extra staff.

Standing out there in the middle and waiting for the sign

from the pavilion to set up the stumps, glancing around at the massed stands and terraces, I never cease to be amazed at the thought of how much preparation has gone into the staging of the match.

And when I have surrendered the wicket to the umpires, I am in sole charge of it up to that point, other thoughts pop into my mind as I retreat to my seat by the sightscreen.

Among those figures in immaculate white trotting so light-heartedly on to the field are a tangle of hopes, ambitions and fears. One of them has a busted thumb, heavily plastered. Will it stand up to that first savage square-cut? Another, a bowler, has had a strained back. How will it feel after a dozen overs at full stretch? Then there is the question of lost form. I know that one of them is particularly worried about it. If he doesn't recover it over the next few days, make an impression one way or another, will it mean that he goes out of the side for good?

All of them have been playing regularly for their counties, all of them have practised assiduously and had fitness tests but no amount of going through the motions and thinking through possible deficiencies of technique can help a man once he is out there before that huge expectant crowd.

Cricket is so much a matter of reflexes, of split-second decisions. And if a player has too much on his mind a vital catch can be muffed, no-balls bowled, the bat waved indecisively to a late swinging ball.

The only criticism in all this build-up that comes my way – apart from the general impression that the ground-staff boys and I positively enjoy rushing out the covers and then delaying the resumption when the rain stops – is that too little information is conveyed over the public address system.

I think this comes mainly from people who are not too conversant with cricket. It is usually when the umpires and players walk off the field because the light is too bad for play to continue – or when these spectators have found out the reason for the stoppage and, seeing a glimmer of sun through the clouds, are outraged that the game is not resumed immediately.

Well, they may have a point. Sometimes the light doesn't

seem all that bad. Was the introduction of light-meters for the umpires really such a good idea?

But spectators and TV viewers may have noticed that in recent Test series the umpires have been out on the field very soon after a break for bad light, so that they could be seen to be judging whether the light had improved.

Most of the complaints in the past have been that in some cases nothing was seen of the umpires for ten or fifteen minutes although, of course, they could have been considering whether play could be resumed from a vantage point in the pavilion.

Throughout this book I have probably said quite enough about the differing views on what is and what is not a good wicket. But as Ron Allsopp is a good mate of mine – we worked together for sixteen years at Trent Bridge and he is now head groundsman there – I cannot resist touching on what the Notts captain, Clive Rice, is reported to have said after their ten wickets' win over Glamorgan which gave them the County Championship in 1981.

He refuted the suggestion that the Trent Bridge wickets had been kept 'green' to enable Richard Hadlee and himself to get their opponents out fairly cheaply. He had happened to be very lucky in winning the toss in the home games and it was his policy to put the visitors in – a policy that had certainly paid off. But his off-spinner, Eddie Hemmings, had collected more wickets at home than away so how could the Nottingham table be called merely a fast bowler's paradise?

No groundsman, however experienced he may be, is infallible. His preparation can go wrong. And when that is the case, there is little he can do about it in the weeks leading up to a Test match, which these days seems to be the occasion for cricket buffs to talk of little else but how the wicket has betrayed the batsmen. The Headingley wicket, blamed for so many dismissals, didn't seem to worry Ian Botham or Graham Dilley overmuch.

During Surrey's marvellous seven-year run of holding the County Championship pennant one heard that the wickets were specially prepared to suit their great spinners, Jim Laker and Tony Lock. And, as you will have gathered, I am quite used to jovial hints from overseas stars that I strive to deaden the Lord's Test wickets to cut down the effectiveness of their battery of fast bowlers.

But, believe me, it would be extremely difficult to prepare wickets specifically for this or that bowling or batting strength; nor would you be encouraged to do so by the authorities. Before the start of each season we do get our instructions but these are simply to implement the desire of everyone in the first-class game for cricket to be played on surfaces that are fast and true enough to maintain an even balance between batsmen and bowlers.

Some wickets may not last as well as they should, and I grant you this must be laid at the groundsman's door, but it is always possible for spinners to get something out of a pitch that has been played on for two days or more. Everyone recognizes this. And when there is any juice at all in the pitch, you can bet that a first-class seamer will exploit it to the full. With swing bowling the weather plays a part and even a Lord's groundsman has no direct line to the mischievous gods who suddenly blanket the skies or whip up a cross-wind.

The basic peculiarities of the Lord's square are scarcely a new topic. In reporting on the activities of 'the Marylebone Club' in his *Cricketers' Companion for 1869*, John Lillywhite wrote:

'Many minor improvements were effected by the committee, and due regard being had to the exceptionally dry weather, the ground "played well", though the season may not be without its "cricket curiosities", as will appear hereafter.'

Incidentally, he also recorded that in 1864 'the Marylebone Club, at an expense of £11,000, purchased from Mr J.H. Dark, the remaining portion (29 years) of the lease of Lord's ground; and also obtained, at an increased rental, from the ground landlord, Mr Moses, an extension of the lease for 70 years; and thus, for 99 years to come, have the Marylebone Club secured, for Cricket and Cricketers, the world-renowned Lord's Ground'.

And further: 'During the past year a very commodious

grand stand has been erected on the upper side of the ground, which commands a good view of the game. On the occasion of the Eton and Harrow, and the University matches, this extensive building was filled to repletion with the "upper ten" who appeared thoroughly to appreciate the excellent accommodation provided by the Directors, who, as a *quid pro quo*, netted a very handsome dividend . . . the number of the "fourth estate" having convenient benches allotted for their use, a circumstance unknown, until 1867, at Lord's.'

Some people, especially Surrey supporters, may feel that in 112 years the prevailing atmosphere at Lord's has not really changed.

As to the 'cricket curiosities' that Lillywhite promised us 'hereafter', one of them was the three-day match between the North and South of the Thames which folded up in one day. 'An event,' wrote Lillywhite, 'we believe, unprecedented.' The North scored 73 and 56, the South 106 and 25. Was the wicket to blame? 'A smart shower during the North's first innings caused the ball to "kick", ' is all we are told.

Ninety-five years later, in his book *Talk of the Double*, Fred Titmus, the England off-spinner who was still turning out in the occasional game for Middlesex in 1980, when he was forty-eight, wrote:

'I am glad I play half my cricket at the great ground in St John's Wood, even though the wicket is not my favourite to bowl on. I like flat wickets for preference. The slight slope across the ground, and the notorious ridge, can be exploited by some bowlers, and I have certainly had my successes on it, but I think I often bowl better away from Lord's.'

But he adds: 'For sheer atmosphere there is no ground to come anywhere near it.'

And ridge or no ridge, slope or no slope, the batsmen are legion who have made towering innings on the Lord's square. A present-day master, Viv Richards of West Indies and Somerset, in an interview by Peter Smith for the *Daily Mail*, was asked about his memorable performances at Lord's.

He replied: 'When I was a lad back in Antigua I used to listen about Lord's, read about batsmen walking down the pavilion steps, pushing their way through that little white gate and stepping on to the outfield.

'I dreamed then that I would do it one day, and the thought of going through that white gate inspires me even now, whether playing for the West Indies or Somerset.

'Something comes over me. It's a special place, the atmosphere is right, the crowds fantastic.'

'A special place. . . .' That was what Ted Swannell had called it when urging me to apply for the job. And that is what it is. Lordly and rather aloof as befits its name, but the only place to be if you love cricket. Everyone comes here.

About ten years ago the Easter coaching classes were on when I encountered an elderly couple, obviously tourists, wandering towards the practice ground. They must have been given permission to look around.

The woman was on her own, her husband a little distance away poising his camera to capture yet another aspect of the ground.

I introduced myself, we exchanged greetings and from her accent it was not difficult to guess that she was Australian.

'You're a long way from home,' I said.

She nodded but her smile was a little strained.

'We're flying back this weekend. I thought it would do him good to see something of the world. We've done France and Italy and – oh, all over. And we've spent an awful lot of money. Too much, I suppose. Because it doesn't seem to have done him much good.'

Then she gave me a sharper look.

'You're not a Londoner either.'

I told her she was quite right. I came from Nottingham . . . Robin Hood, lace, Trent Bridge, another big cricket ground.

'Trent Bridge!' she cried. And she called to her husband to join us.

'Trent Bridge,' she said as he came up, 'Mr Fairbrother, he looks after the ground here, but he comes from Trent Bridge.'

'Trent Bridge,' he echoed, and I had never heard it said with such reverence, 'what, you worked there?'

I nodded.

'Then you knew Harold Larwood and Bill Voce.'

'I saw them play,' I said, 'but I was a bit young.'

I saw that he was digging into his overcoat pocket. He drew out a battered card and waved it at me. 'See that? Scorecard – Sydney Oval – bodyline series. But I don't care what they said, the papers. You had a great side then. Fine bunch of chaps.'

'Would you like to meet Bill Voce?' I said.

'*Meet* him . . .' He just gazed at me.

I pointed to the distant nets.

'The tall man with the youngsters. That's Bill Voce.'

'Voce . . . you're pulling my leg.'

'You sit down here,' I said, gesturing to one of the benches, 'and I'll bring him over to you.'

He was literally gasping.

'Voce . . . Bill Voce. Tried to get his autograph – end of play – when they came off – round by the dressing rooms. Couldn't get near him.'

Well, they did meet, and they talked, with Bill just as keen as his companion to reminisce about that famous series.

Before I left them, his wife drew me aside.

'You don't know what this means for us – for him. Look at his face. He's like a boy. I haven't seen him like that for years. He's been a sick man, you know. He still is.' I felt a gentle pressure on my hand. 'We shan't be here again. But this is enough. He's happy, really happy just now. That's all I wanted. Bless this place.'

Yes, Lord's is very special.

# PART II
## *GRASS ROOTS*

# 1

# THE SPRING PROGRAMME

Scarification is a very important job in the spring. All fine turf areas will respond to gentle scarification aimed at lifting straggly material from the sole of the turf. But if you are using a roto-rake and not a hand wire rake, do resist the temptation to set the machine for a deep cut.

This light scarification should be carried out during a period of good growing weather with the blades of the machine set so that they will just flick through the sward.

The rotorake, in particular, drags out the thatch and any weeds and allows the air to get to the roots of your grass. This type of work – again, lightly done – is absolutely essential for your cricket table. For the larger area of your outfield use a light chain harrow if you have one. To wire-rake it by hand is hard work indeed.

Aeration scarifying may not seem to be a very rewarding operation at the time but it certainly gets the turf off to a good start and later, when you come to prepare wickets, you will be delighted to see clean, even tracks.

Next in importance is the application of a spring fertilizer dressing.

The aim should be to provide a balanced feed which will encourage natural growth. It is wrong to try to force growth in the early spring. And be careful with your timing. We groundsmen dread being caught out by a mild spell of weather followed by a period of biting cold. That cold snap could severely damage a soft lush growth resulting from fertilizer applied too early.

It will vary from region to region but mid-April is usually

considered to be a good time for the spring dressing.

What should this dressing consist of? Well, at Lord's we use a compound of which the main constituents are nitrogen, phosphates and potash.

*Nitrogen* (N) controls the rate of plant growth and is responsible for the leaf development and intensity of coloration.

*Phosphates* (P) promote root growth.

*Potash* (K) improves the health and vigour of the plant enabling it to withstand adverse conditions of soil, climate and disease.

These are the three essential plant nutrients which any crop requires and since most soils do not supply them in sufficient quantity, this is where fertilizers come in.

We use a compound fertilizer which is a combination of all three. A *straight* fertilizer of nitrogen would contain sulphate of ammonia, nitrate of soda and dried blood; that of phosphates – superphosphate and bone meal; that of potash – sulphate of potash, muriate of potash and wood ash.

Bulk organic manures, such as farmyard manure or spent hops, can be considered as low-value compound fertilizers but with the additional benefit of being a source humus to the soil.

A cautionary word. The machines and chemicals used in turf culture should be treated with the greatest care. Protective clothing should always be worn. Few chemicals can be claimed to be completely harmless. Keep them under lock and key.

As spring progresses your mower comes into greater use. The grass is getting stronger and needs cutting more frequently. but keep the cut at your winter height in order to maintain a neat and tidy appearance. Be patient and keep the cut at that height till the growth becomes more settled – not till then should you lower the cut.

And remember to brush before mowing. This lifts up any straggly stems and also disperses worm casts.

I shouldn't have to say it, but do check that the materials and machinery you need for each process are on hand and in good order ready to get to work quickly and efficiently. Particularly if you are a spare-time or volunteer groundsman it will only waste the hours and vex you to have to make frequent trips from pitch to shed and back again!

# 2

# PREPARING THE TABLE FOR YOUR WICKETS

Actual pitch preparation basically involves raking, mowing and rolling, and it is imperative to roll only when the conditions are right for it. For instance, rolling when there is too much moisture in the top can make a wicket quite unplayable.

The average cricket club has only one main roller but county clubs usually have a series of rollers of varying weights which they can use in the early spring in sequence to firm up the table. After this, rolling is confined to the preparation of individual pitches.

Never rush your rolling stints. Easy does it and then there won't be any damage to the soil structure or the grasses. And surface aeration regularly about twice a week will keep air penetrating the soil and maintain a high growth rate in the table.

At Lord's we start with the motor mower which rolls and tops the grass at the same time, then an 8cwt roller for the first day. On the second day we put on the 18cwt. If the weather is right we go on rolling for about five hours each day – slowly and carefully, of course. After about four weeks of this we bring on the motor roller, the real heavy, 36cwt, for the final rolling over just one day. This is followed by a good surface aeration of the table and what one might call the brush-off.

Any kind of rolling must be foreign to the very nature of grass which has the drive to rise through air and moisture to the sun, and that is why I have laid such stress on the right and wrong times to trundle out that roller. Soil compaction deprives the grass roots of air and impairs drainage. Intensive spiking is always needed to counteract the inevitable compaction of all sports turf soils, especially those of cricket tables.

Now is the time to bring out your set square and begin squaring out your table. To do this, stretch a thin cord or string line the full length of the table along what is intended to be the bowler's crease at one end of all the proposed wickets. Then, at a right angle to this first line, stretch a line spot 22 yards, being the distance between the two sets of stumps when set up for play.

To make sure the distance between the two stump settings is precisely correct a wicket chain or steel tape should be used. (For the benefit of those who are no longer taught the Imperial measure, a chain is exactly 22 yards.)

Having laid down the two lines in the correct positions, at a true right angle, it is easy to complete the job. To make this permanent, remove a small plug of turf on your squaring marks – the holes should be about two inches wide and two inches deep – and then fill in with whiting. This will last throughout the season.

It is then a matter of stretching your line from the corner spots along the bowler's crease and the line of the stumps, and measuring an equal distance from one wicket to the next, at the same time keeping all the wickets in a straight line all season.

Not only does a properly squared off table look neat and professional, but it makes the cutting of each fresh wicket so much easier for the groundsman.

To minimize wear or damage to your square at the start of the season it is wise to prepare the wicket for your first match near the edge of the table and work across as the season progresses. I like to have from ten to fourteen days' preparation on wickets before they are actually needed for play.

# 3

# PREPARING THE WICKET

In the routine procedure of maintenance the table would have been wormed earlier in the year, firmed by rolling in March and April and would then be ready for actual match preparation.

This having been done, mow the turf once, twice or more, if necessary, to remove the bulk of the grass, then scarify the surface of the wicket, making sure not to disturb the soil surface. Only the grass is roughed up by the scarifying by machine or hand rake.

After this, mow again until you are satisfied enough grass has been removed – this is the art of groundsmanship! – but don't mow too close at this early stage. Little and often is the watchword. A certain amount of rolling will still be required to firm the wicket and although this heavy weight might produce one satisfactory strip, the process could well make it unusable later in the season. Always remember that grass is a living, breathing plant and suffers from being too compressed or caked.

Having satisfied yourself that you have made a good wicket you have to decide whether the surface is damp enough to a few inches in depth or needs watering. Moisture is essential to plant life but it should be timed to fit in with play, bearing in mind that cricket is best played on a dry surface. Ensure that watering is commenced in good time so that the reserves of water in the soil are never exhausted but rather maintained at a suitable level. Once turf dries out it can be extremely difficult to revive. The aim should be to allow sufficient moisture below to feed the grass roots.

The first rolling lays the foundation of a good or a bad wicket. If there is too much water near the surface the weight of rolling produces a dirty black strip after the first or second time over it. Yet it is essential at this stage of pitch preparation for the surface and subsoil to be damp to a depth of a few inches, otherwise your rolling will be ineffective.

At no time should rolling be attempted when water is visible on the surface of the wicket.

Every soil in every part of the country has its own quality or disadvantages and I shall be dealing with this later.

One further tip on watering. Never sprinkle water on a parched surface. This could be disastrous for both your wicket and the players. A ball pitching on a damp patch deflects quite nastily. When you water, always flood the entire wicket so that the water gets down into the subsoil to a depth of at least four inches. Then wait your time before rolling again.

After taking the roller off your wicket inspect the track for any faults. Any small holes, perhaps made by the heel of a boot, cannot be rolled out. Gently prise them up with a knife or an old screwdriver around the edge of the damage, and press back into place with the handle.

Look particularly at the area at both ends where the ball usually pitches, that is about three to six yards in front of the batsman's or popping crease. Once you are satisfied that you have dealt satisfactorily with these holes or dents, give the wicket some more rolling while it is still damp.

Sun and wind are the great healers and it is amazing how a wicket dries out in this kind of weather.

There is always the fear that the wicket will break up if the sun lasts and it becomes almost too dry, but if you have applied the right top dressing in the autumn and chosen the grass species to suit your particular soil, you should not be too afraid of this happening.

Mow the wicket at intervals up to match day and roll again if you think it is still a little damp. Wickets play poorly for quite different reasons. It could be due to preparation being done too late; insufficient watering; the roller put on at the wrong time; or not allowing the wicket to dry out into a good, easy-paced pitch. Unfortunately, the snags are many, which is probably why groundsmanship is now a respected profession!

I suppose more wickets are spoilt by over-rolling than anything else, particularly when the roller has been used on a fairly hard surface that has had a slight shower.

On the morning of the match, in addition to marking out the wicket, and for this you should have line markers and a brush that will give you elegant creases that make such a difference to the final appearance, shave the grass and give the strip one more rolling before the captains spin up.

If you are fortunate enough to be able to cover your wicket against rain, be content to protect just the bowlers' and batsmen's creases. The rest of the pitch is best left open. Flat plastic sheets cause the turf to sweat and draw moisture to the surface so that again you might get damp spots on a length.

A word to the trainee groundsman about a dusty wicket.

This means the crumbling of the pitch, usually three to six yards in front of the batsman's crease, so that when the ball pitches it digs into the surface and brings up puffs of dust. From this the ball deflects from its true flight (erratic bounce is another way of putting it) and to say that it makes batting difficult is an understatement. In county cricket when wickets break up like this fairly regularly the county will often take its fixtures away from the ground.

If only certain strips are affected these must be taken out of play until they have been treated. A strong turf cover must be established as soon as possible. Groundsmen have their own preference as to whether this should be done by seeding or turfing. If successful repairs are to be achieved by seeding the work should be done by mid-September at the latest.

The bare and thin areas should be carefully scarified, preferably with a rotorake. Take it both down and across the bad parts of the wicket, doing it lightly all the time, then mow and solid tine the areas. At Lord's we use a spiked roller called a Sorrel. Then sow a fine seed mixture at the rate determined by the turf density. Follow this up with a light application of screened top dressing just enough to cover the seed.

Dusty patches with practically no grass at all are best re-turfed but this needs particular care and, as I have mentioned before, entails maintaining a turf nursery that has been tended as conscientiously as the cricket table itself.

# 4

# THE SOIL AND ITS IMPORTANCE

A major factor governing the maintenance and treatment of your cricket table is the type of soil with which you or your groundsman is coping. For instance, it is more than difficult to produce hard, fast and true wickets on a sandy soil. Either a special soil has to be imported if you are making a new cricket table or you must use top dressings of an imported clay loam soil.

But we have to be clear as to what we mean by clay loam. Often silts are confused with clays and such soils will only hold together if they contain sufficient moisture. When dry – and we know that wickets must be dry to be anything near true and fast – silts are liable to disintegrate.

Fortunately for groundsmen of today there are practical tests which can be carried out to determine whether a soil has sufficient binding qualities. There are many kinds of loam that can be categorized into various groups. Many groundsmen are not in a position to be able to test the sand, silt and clay properties of their soil, but there are establishments to which they can send samples of their soil for analysis, and thus obtain the right top dressing.

Clay loam topsoil is certainly to be favoured as a top dressing but, in the absence of this, a proportion of up to 20 to 30 per cent marl could (before application) be incorporated with the heaviest topsoil available so as to achieve the right amount of strength in your basic soil.

The right soils for cricket will have clay content of 30 to 40 per cent and the clay will be stabilised by association with organic matter so that it will be in good heart to favour healthy growth of grass when the pitch is not in use.

The groundsman must aim at producing a strong, flat surface, so the essentials must be the right soil and the right treatment in preparing the wickets.

# 5

# RENNOVATION OF WINTER PITCHES

When April comes around it is time to patch up the damage as a season's play will have created compacted topsoil, at least in the inch or two below the surface; and where the grass cover has been lost this compaction tends to go deeper in places. So to give the surviving grasses and those to be sown the best chance of rapid establishment, the first thing to be done is to relieve the compaction.

Where the grass cover is good much can be achieved by very intensive spiking, making passes in different directions with a deep slitter, on the bare parts the soil may need cultivating thoroughly. To break up the hard ground, small areas can easily be done with a garden fork or small rake, but for a quick job on larger areas a disc harrow or tilther rake should be used.

Rotavators are also effective for this work. Try to get about 4 inches deep in the ground, and I mean a steady 4 inches because the ground must be kept level at all times.

Many pitches end the season in a sea of mud. To be blunt, the reason for this is poor drainage. When a table gets into this state is needs drastic treatment – and quickly. Get to work just as soon as your last game has been played.

Poor drainage can be due to a number of factors but mainly:

(1) the subsoil is insufficiently permeable and lacks a till drainage system;

(2) the nature of the topsoil prevents water percolation.

Now what can be done about your messy pitch?

Well, the solutions are many. They range from till drainage through sand slitting, sand grooving, subsoiling, mole ploughing, annual sand top dressing. If the problems get worse it really is worth getting experts on the drainage of sports pitches to give you their opinion. And usually it is worth acting on it.

When the cultivations are completed, get the grasses sown right away as the longer they have to establish themselves the better the results will be at the start of the new season.

The choice of grass seeds depends on the sport for which the pitch is used. For soccer and rugby, perennial ryegrass is the species to go for and there are several good cultivators on the market bred for turf use and with high tolerance of wear. When a fine, fairly close-cut sward is required – for hockey or cricket outfields, for example – fescues bent smooth-stalked meadow grass is often used. In recent years dwarf ryegrasses have also proved suitable for such pitches.

Seed can be broadcast by hand or with an autoseeder. In the latter case make passes in different directions using small amounts. The degree of success in your sowing will depend greatly on the weather so try to make sure it is finished before the end of May.

When the grasses show, allow them to grow up to two or three inches before the first cut, then just top regularly during the summer to allow them to thicken. Too close a cut, especially in a very hot spell, causes browning and weakening of the blades. It is also necessary to apply a light dressing of fertilizer to get a good established sward before mid-August. Then, if the drainage is working properly, and you have done your preparation thoroughly, you won't have to keep your fingers too tightly crossed!

# 6

# CRICKET GROUNDSMANSHIP: MONTH BY MONTH

## JANUARY

Depending upon the local weather, this can be a busy month, making full use of your aerating equipment, whether slitting or hollow or solid tining on the same machine, all this can only bring most beneficial results to your square and outfield. Brush and harrow often to prevent thatch.

If the field is also used for winter sport, make haste to repair any deep scars with forking around them and pressing the sides together.

Check on the draining system and correct any faults.

On a good open day, preferably with no wind, so that the fertilizing powder being used is distributed evenly, do some worm killing to keep them in control.

## FEBRUARY

Keep up the brushing and aerating. This operation is most beneficial now the winter is passing.

Again if the weather is dry and mild, this is the time for any turfing. Done at this time it will lead to natural root development before the top growth is too advanced.

And if the surface is practically dry, which can happen in February (May and June are often wetter, as we cricketers know to our cost!) set the mowing machine high and tip the table. *Remember* never to cut low this early in the season.

## MARCH

This is the month when the pitch needs to be rolled after the winter weather. But you will have to judge for yourself when the conditions are right for the first rolling and brushing. To roll a pitch at an inappropriate time may well do more harm than good, so make sure the day and the ground conditions are favourable.

Rolling at the wrong time is just as harmful as using a wicket at the wrong time.

And don't forget the brushing on the square and outfield, this lifts recumbent grass stems. A light rolling firms the table. I like to use my 36-inch motor mower which tips the blades and rolls at the same time.

If the conditions are still and moist, most areas will benefit from a spring fertilizer at this time.

APRIL

Now that you have begun the firming of the table, and if the weather is still kind, keeping dry and with no frost at nights, start getting bigger weights on. And always, *always*, remember to *finish* your rolling on the line of play, from bowler to batsman. Cross mowing and rolling can be done on the outfield as on the square.

Spiking and brushing should follow the rolling session – it promotes a healthy surface, working in any top dressing that is lying around.

If you have the time and the help, give the matted parts of the outfield a thorough scarification – with rake and brush or mechanically.

MAY

More regular mowing is the watchword of this month. Lower the height of cut as the month advances and, if possible, box the cuttings. At Lord's we box the cuttings on the square and outfield at all times as it helps to stop weeds spreading. There are different opinions on this and for garden lawns a high cut, even at this time of year, will produce a full sward and for people who, perhaps, cannot afford fertilizer, the cuttings at least give back some nitrogen to the grass.

Spring sowing. This necessitates harrowing the worn areas to loosen the compacted surface. The grass seed should be raked into the surface and, if possible, it should be covered with some light loamy soil for the outfield. On the table, however, use a heavy clay loam. Never, never, a light sandy loam for your square. It won't hold up to use.

When sowing has been done in March or April, it may be necessary this month carefully to remove any perennial weeds or coarse grasses before they become firmly established. As I say, the work should be done carefully to minimise surface disturbance. Grass is alive and breathing. At this stage treat it like a nurse would a patient!

But weed-killing operations are extremely important. The usual variable May weather encourages rosette and creeping weeds – such troublesome species as the clovers, parsley pint, pearlwort, dandelions and daisies.

Don't mow for three or four days prior to spraying and leave the turf unmown for the same period afterwards. In drought conditions, however brief, you will have to use the water sprayers.

JUNE

The weather should by now be warm and showery and your healthy grasses are growing. Be on the look-out for the first signs of fungoid attack. *Fuserium* is a white cottony mycelial fungus; and straw-like blades of grass with red cottony attachments will certainly be *corticium fuciforme*. Prompt measures with the right fungicide should bring the trouble under control.

As I have said before, regular brushing and raking make these attacks less likely and also stimulate healthy grass.

If, in the unlikely event, the weather is dry for a week or two, don't forget to raise the height of your cutting machines when mowing the outfield and square. And unless drought regulations floor you, carry on with the watering of both – in the evening, if possible which is always the best time.

About now I like to give a dressing of fertilizer again. Say, 2 oz. per square yard. Water by hand if there is no rain about.

JULY

What I have advised for June in turf management applies to July as well, particularly as regards fungi. This is the month when *fairy* or *puffball rings* occur – always encouraged by wet weather, of course.

Few, if any, fungicides are really effective in controlling these rings. I would advise forking along the fungi about 6 inches deep and applying a solution of sulphate of iron, using

½ oz. in 2 gallons of water per square yard. If, after this, the fairy rings survive, use washing-up liquid – 1 oz. in 2 gallons of water per square yard.

If this fails, dig out the rings, filling in with good sandy loam, then seeding or turfing the place and later working in a little top dressing.

AUGUST

For the counties the cricket season is now coming to a close, thought I am well aware that most club cricketers soldier on through September. But either way, so far as the groundsman is concerned this is the time to start work on the cricket table so that it will preserve its quality for the following season.

As your strips come out of play re-turf the bowlers' ends, or seed them if this suits you better. In the case of turfing it is certainly essential to have maintained a reserve plot of grass as carefully as you have tended the table itself.

The same applies to your practice wickets. If these are neglected your batsmen will have a rough time at the start of next season when they most need a true and even bounce for their stroke play.

Make every effort to complete your renovation of the table so that the treatment may become effective before winter sets in. Deep aeration is important at this time after all the heavy wear and the frequent use of the roller. And I find it a good policy to sow grass seed between all the creases at the same time as I am re-turfing. This oversowing strengthens the sward.

SEPTEMBER

Carrying through from August, you should be making use of every opportunity to finish your re-turfing and seeding of the table.

Thorough scarification of the outfield is necessary and continue the aerating process, choosing the milder, moister days. This is also a good month for worm control and dealing with the leather-jacket (crane-fly) grubs before they can do any damage to the root system of the grasses. Chlordane (granules or liquid) is ideal for both purposes. It checks leather-jackets for around four years and worms for at least two seasons.

Prompt treatment with a suitable turf fungicide is your weapon against all kind of invaders. And don't neglect the brushing or caning of the dewy grass in the early morning. This removes the surface conditions favoured by disease.

OCTOBER

The turfing and seeding having been done, you should now spike the square and put a top dressing of heavy clay loam all over it. The quantity works out at about 4lb per sq yd per string. Assuming you have set strings in sections 36yd long and a yard wide, it is a barrowload for each section. To distribute the loam evenly, use a lute (a narrow board on the end of a broom handle) or drag brush.

While the weather remains favourable (on average, October is a mild, pleasant month) keep up the aerating and brushing of your outfield.

NOVEMBER/DECEMBER

It is now that any damage caused by the crane-fly grub – leather-jackets – may become visible. Where they are at work your grass will be a poor colour and another sure sign of their presence will be flocks of starlings, digging away with their sharp beaks. What can you do about it? Disturb the patches with rake or brush and, where necessary, start again from stage one, seed or turf, top-dress.

When there is frost on the ground or a fall of snow, leave it be. Already the young grasses are just forming and it does no good to have feet flatten them. Of course this applies particularly to the table though, if you are wise, you will have fenced it round for the winter.

This is a rest period so far as ground treatment is concerned. Stay inside and get all your equipment cleaned and mended ready for next season.

# 7

# PESTS AND FUNGUS DISEASES

**Pests**

*Chafer grubs.* White fleshy grubs with brown heads and curved bodies. They feed on the grass roots and cause withered patches to appear.

*Earthworms.* Two species of worm are responsible for depositing casts on the surface of turf. They are particularly active during the spring and autumn.

*Leather-jackets.* The greyish brown or greyish black larvae of the crane-fly with tough, wrinkled skin. These also feed on the roots of grass, causing it to wither. The damage occurs in the spring and late summer and is at its worst if the preceding winter has been wet.

All these pests are active in the surface soil, therefore pesticides must be of the long-lasting type. The pests will either come into contact with treated soil or consume treated soil or vegetation.

*Chafer grubs* and *leather-jackets* are easily controlled by DDT, BHC or chlordane; *earthworms* by the older methods of mownah meal or lead arsenate, or chlordane, the newer chemical. Chlordane, in fact, is effective against all turf pests, and if applied annually at the correct dosage will give you complete pest control after a single spraying. This is obviously a great boon to us groundsmen since the presence of pests such as leather-jackets is seldom apparent until the damage is done. A classic case of prevention being better than cure.

**Fungus diseases**

*Dollar spot.* Small brown patchess about three inches

across, only brown at first, then developing a rather bleached appearance.

*Fairy rings.* In summer the ring is composed of three zones, thc outer and inner rings consisting of green and vigorous grass while in the middle ring the grass is brown and killed by the fairy ring fungus.

*Red thread.* This disease is outlined in distinct patches three to fifteen inches in diameter. A red hornlike fungus growth can be seen emerging from leaf sheaths and bridging from leaf to leaf. The leaves become darkened and wet.

*Snow mould or fuserium patch.* Large brown patches, most damage caused under melting snow or by early spring rains. The dying leaves have a pink tint because of the spores. The fringe of killed patches may have a pink mould growth when the disease is active.

Relative to this, when your cricket table is covered with snow I would advise you to leave it. By clearing away the snow you would almost certainly damage the turf and leave it exposed to frost. The snow, in fact, acts as a protective blanket. If, after the snow has melted and you spot a disease such as fuserium take prompt action. And when the ground has thawed out completely, remember that considerable damage can be caused by walking or working on it.

## Control methods

The standard treatments for turf diseases are the two Mercury Compounds Mercurous Chloride (Calomel) and Mercuric Chloride (Corrosive Sublimate) and again, preventive measures should be applied immediately the disease is apparent. Correct feeding will do much to make grass resistant to these diseases and the control of moss, which I mean to deal with at greater length, also involves the use of Mercury Compounds. Their effect is long-lasting and an annual treatment of turf with Mercurous Chloride in late summer or autumn is good maintenance.

A thorough knowledge of the use of chemicals for weed control is a vital part of groundsmanship.

For broad-leaved weeds like clovers, pearlwort and many

small-leaved weeds, 2, 4-D MCDA dichlenprop, fenoprop and toxynil mecoprop can be recommended. These may be available as straight weed-killers but to give broad spectrum weed-killers the manufacturers combine two or more of the above chemicals so that a single spraying will control virtually all weed growth present.

When using such chemicals three factors should be considered at all times.

(1) You must adhere to the recommended application rate. Too little and the weed will not be killed. Too much and scorching of the grass will occur.

(2) Before application, your equipment should be checked. See that the spray tank and tubes are clean and not contaminated from the previous spraying. This could be very serious if the chemical last used was a total week-killer such as Simazine when the job in hand is to apply selective weed-killers on your actual cricket table. So always wash your equipment thoroughly after use.

(3) Relative to the second factor, check that spraying nozzles are clean and not cracked or chipped so that the correct spray pattern is being formed. Check that pressure controls are set to what is required and likewise with the spreaders, which must be absolutely clean. Ensure that the adjustable and setting levers are secure so that there will be no vibration when the machine is in operation.

So the equipment has been filled and now you start applying the chemical. This should always be carried out methodically. Use markers as a guide to the areas that have been covered and those yet to be treated. Wheel marks of your tractor or spraying machine or spreader are ideal for lining up each time.

And don't forget that weather conditions are important to the success of your spraying. Stop work immediately if they are unsuitable.

**Moss**

Actual invasion of the turf by moss usually occurs when the grass is not growing actively and is less competitive. For instance it can happen where the grass is shaded or because of inadequate fertilization or poor drainage or the grass having been cut too closely.

If you are in any doubt as to the main cause, be sensible and send some soil samples to the Sports Turf Research Institute in Bingley, West Yorkshire. Their experts will soon tell you what the trouble is and how it can be tackled.

There are many different types of moss and identification is not easy. The first essential is to be able to recognize moss and not confuse it with other weeds which may demand quite different methods of control, for instance, with pearlwort (*Vagina procumbens*), which is dark green and a close mat at the lowest level of the sward.

The three main types of moss are:

(1) A trailer with branched stems (e.g., *Eurhynchium praelongum*).

(2) Numerous small, upright stems closely packed together and forming a slightly raised patch (e.g., *Ceratadon purpureus*).

(3) One with larger, upright, fairly tall stems not so closely packed as (2) and with its individual leaves stiff and clearly visible on the stem (e.g., *Polytrichum juniperinum*).

Moss, although quite attractive in appearance on cottage lawns, must be considered a weed and on cricket grounds its eradication is essential for good grass growth. We use lawn sands and mercury compounds to control it. Lawn sands which have mercurial additives are usually the cheapest but are not very long-lasting in effect. Mercury compounds are effective for up to twelve months and since they are also fungicides they constitute an insurance against both moss and turf fungus.

Having said that, the best treatment is the removal of the conditions which have allowed the moss to thrive.

# 8

# NON-TURF PITCHES

In the last few years the research into suitable subsitutes for a grass wicket has come on apace. More and morc clubs and schools and local authorities are putting down artificial wickets either for net practice or for actual match play.

Of course matting wickets have been in use for a long time. In hot countries they have been absolutely essential since no grasses can stand up to long months of sizzling heat.

Our own situation is quite the reverse. Almost anywhere in the British Isles we suffer from what is technically called 'a temperate climate' but is, from the cricketer's point of view, a cloud cover that holds in its fist downpours of rain which are sometimes cloaked by the weather forecasters as 'occasional showers'.

The non-turf pitch dries out quicker than grass after rain so that is one reason for its increasing popularity.

Next, there is the question of maintenance. Good groundsmen are scarce. And if you can get one, he is now able to ask for a living wage. It was very different in the past when he had to be satisfied with being treated very much as a labourer and paid accordingly.

But of course the small village club, the school with its local council ever more pressed to keep down the rates, may not be able to afford an experienced groundsman who will certainly have to live on or near the ground and devote every working day to the proper maintenance of square and outfield. Therefore the outlay on the construction of a non-turf wicket will undoutedly be a sensible alternative, with voluntary help to keep the wicket surrounds and outfield in something like fair condition.

Not an ideal solution, I must stress, but a means of continuing to play good cricket instead of having to abandon the game in favour of one that does not demand an even surface such as baseball or softball.

To put the whole thing in perspective, whereas a grass cricket square needs a groundsman who can plan how to prepare enough strips to take the requisite number of games, and do all the necessary nurturing and treatment of the turf, the artificial wicket is hard-wearing enough for all the season's matches to be played on it. And it will always be true and level so long as it is treated well and the base has been truly laid.

**Artificial surfaces**

| *Type of pitch* | *Base* | *Playing surface* |
|---|---|---|
| Permanent | Concrete | Astroturf |
| | Concrete | Bituturf |
| Pitch remains in situ | Concrete | Semtex |
| | Concrete or asphalt | Tartan |
| Surface fixed to base | Concrete | |
| Temporary playing | Any type of base or surface | Recticel<br>Ruberoid |
| These surfaces can | Wood | Tartan |
| be fixed or lifted | Asphalt | Truturf |
| and stored away after use | Wood | Universal Mat |

Generally speaking, most of the materials currently on the market, when laid on a hard base, have a higher bounce than turf. Consequently, there is a tendency for the ball to bounce too much for the slow bowler and the wrist spinner will turn it too much. On the other hand, the medium-pace bowler will make the ball rise stump high. So if the base is not free of grit or dirt when the matting is laid the playing characteristics will vary. Clean up or bounce up!

*Astroturf* (St Mary's Landscape, Sussex Way, London NW19)

Hard-wearing

Produces an easy-paced pitch.

Average amount of spin.

Occasional brushing and washing. Otherwise, no maintenance required.

*Bituturf* (En Tout Cas Ltd, Syston, Leicester LE7 8NP)

Takes more spin than a turf pitch and the ball tends to lift sharply.

Will last for years provided it is laid correctly and regularly maintained.

Inclined to mark playing equipment due to the nature of the material.

*Recticel* (Sutcliffe Recticel Ltd, 18-22 Summerville Road, Bradford, Yorkshire BDY 1PY)

Produces an easy-paced pitch.

Rather too much spin, perhaps more than on turf.

No maintenance required. Just roll it up and put it away after play, particularly when used out-of-doors.

*Ruberoid* (Ruberoid Co. Ltd, Commonwealth House, 1 New Oxford Street, London WC1A 1PE)

A true fast pitch, the ball coming through stump high.

Surface takes a little spin but the ball tends to bounce too much for the slow bowler.

No maintenance required. Just keep the base smooth, hard and free from dirt.

*Semtex* (Dunlop Semtex Ltd, 19-20 Berner Street, London W1)

Medium-fast pitch, the ball seldom rising above stump high for the pace bowler.

Difficult to spin the ball on this surface.

Very hard-wearing and can be repaired easily.

No preparation or maintenance.

*Tartan* (3M Co. Ltd, 3M House, Wigmore Street, London W1A 1ET)

Produces an easy-paced pitch, the ball seldom rising stump high; difficult for the fast bowler to deliver effective bouncers.

The surface takes too much spin, particularly of the wristy kind.

Very hard-wearing.

More acceptable on concrete.

No maintenance or preparation required.

*Truturf* (En Tout Cas Ltd, Syston, Leicester LE7 8NP)

A fast-paced pitch for the seam bowler. The ball rises at least stump high for the fast bowler who could be hostile.

Takes too much spin. The ball will rise sharply and bounce too much.

Not suitable for outside use. If it is needed outside, don't get it wet. Always store away after use.

No maintenance needed.

*Universal Mat* (Universal Materials Co. Ltd, Brent House, 214 Kenton Road, Kenton, Middlesex)

Matting produces a fast pitch. The ball tends to bounce too much and the spinners turn the ball too sharply and make it lift.

The weave of the laminated rubber strips of which the matting is made might cause the ball to come through at uneven height and pace.

But matting is very durable, and has been used for practice and match cricket for many years and is excellent for bowlers' run-ups.

Always lay it on a clean, flat, true base. No maintenance is required.

# INDEX